Bid Better, Play Better

How To Think at the Bridge Table

by
Dorothy Hayden Truscott

Published by
DEVYN PRESS, INC.
Louisville, Kentucky

Revised and updated edition. Previous edition was
published by Perennial Library in 1986.

Eighth Printing January 2012

Printed in the United States of America.

Devyn Press, Inc.
3600 Chamberlain Lane, Suite 206
Louisville, KY 40241
1-800-274-2221
Fax (502) 426-2044

ISBN 978-0-939460-77-9

Contents

Introduction

by B. Jay Becker

There are all kinds of bridge books being published today, and nearly all are more technical and less interesting than they should be. Few of them contain the sage advice and common sense you will encounter in BID BETTER, PLAY BETTER.

What Dorothy Hayden Truscott does so effectively in this book is to teach you how to think at the bridge table. There is not much point in asking you to memorize a series of general rules unless you understand the logic behind them. You cannot solve a difficult bridge problem by rote. The game is too complicated for that. But you can solve a great many problems if you appreciate the reason for the rule and know whether it applies to the particular situation confronting you.

There is an amazing similarity between the way Mrs. Truscott plays bridge and the way she writes. It may come as a surprise to some to learn that she is the only woman to have represented the United States in the World Championship as a result of having qualified through the annual trials method.

Many men think that women do not have the stamina to meet the relentless and grueling requirements of the Trials or of National or World Championship play but in Dorothy's case I can testify first hand that there is nothing to this contention. If she has a breaking-point I have yet to discover it. Her magnificent record in open events as well as mixed and women's events is well-known. But enough of this flattery of my favorite partner. I won't even mention her impeccably good manners, her fine sense of humor, her good looks, her status as one of the leading bridge mathematicians, or anything else about her because I know you must be awaiting impatiently to read what she has to say about bridge.

PREFACE

When I wrote the first edition of this book in 1965 bidding was both different and simpler. The bridge language we spoke then is about as different from that of today as Shakespearian speech is from that of Hollywood.

A bidding system is a language, and like any other language is continually in transition. This book recommends a style that is halfway between the traditional and the ultra-modern, a style that is easily adopted by the intermediate player without having to add too many artificial gadgets.

For example the strong two bid is today about as obsolete as the buggy whip. Here to stay are:

Five-card majors
Weak two bids
Weak jump overcalls
Limit raises
Negative doubles
Major suit transfer responses to notrump

This book is structured around these. For the intermediate player who wishes to go further, many of the conventions that are popular in tournament play are described in Chapter 11, The Gadgets.

BID BETTER, PLAY BETTER is intended for three groups of readers: the player who has learned the rules and needs to know more; the traditional player who wishes to modernize his, or her, bidding; and the teacher who wishes the student to learn what players actually do today rather than what they did the day before yesterday.

Dorothy Hayden Truscott

1

The World of Bridge

How many bridge players realize that our game, which seems so modern, has a long history behind it.

Playing cards were used in China as long ago as A.D. 979 although, sadly, the legend that they were invented by the Emperor to amuse his concubines has no validity. Some three hundred years later they appeared in Venice, possibly introduced by Marco Polo on his return from China. During the next century they spread rapidly throughout Europe and were well on time to catch the first boat to America. Legend tells us that Columbus's sailors threw their playing cards overboard in superstitious terror during a raging Atlantic storm. Later, on dry land, they regretted their rashness and made new ones out of leaves.

Playing cards reached England early in the fifteenth century and it was here that the ancestor of modern bridge was born. This early game was called variously "triumph," "trump," "ruff and honours," "whisk and swabbers," and "whisk." The earliest recorded reference to the game is in 1529, but it is clear that it had been played long before this.

By the seventeenth century the game, by then called "Whisk" or "whist," had become very popular particularly in London. Just as today, the game was played by four people, the two sitting opposite being partners. Thirteen cards were dealt to each player, and the score was determined by the number of tricks won above and beyond the first six tricks, which became known as the "book."

There was no bidding, and trump was determined by turning up the last card dealt. There was no dummy exposed which made whist much more difficult than bridge. (In case you do not believe this, try playing bridge without a dummy.)

In the coffee-houses of London it was common to have a game of whist in progress with a ring of kibitzers standing around the table anxious to bet with the players or with each other. It resembled a miniature stock exchange, and wagers were laid on anything from the play of a card to whether it would rain tomorrow. It was, in fact, a group of whist players at Edward Lloyd's Coffee House who in their spare time founded the famous Lloyd's of London.

Such was the lively atmosphere when Edmond Hoyle (1672-1769) arrived on the scene. A barrister of good family and education, he became the first professional whist teacher. He wrote the first book devoted to the game and it rapidly became a best seller going through many editions. Much of what he wrote on card play is still applicable today.

Before Hoyle's time even the basic finesse was understood only by experts or those in contact with experts. Now it was available to all. As a result the popularity of the game grew by leaps and bounds, particularly among the ladies and gentlemen of society. Whist had become a highly respected, intellectual pursuit. Hoyle established the tradition of law and order in card-play and the expression "according to Hoyle" became part of the English language.

Perhaps the most famous hand in the entire history of bridge is the one said to have been dealt over two hundred years ago in the gaming rooms at Bath, England, to the Duke of Cumberland.

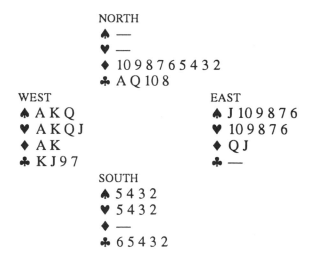

```
                    NORTH
                    ♠ —
                    ♥ —
                    ♦ 10 9 8 7 6 5 4 3 2
                    ♣ A Q 10 8
    WEST                                EAST
    ♠ A K Q                             ♠ J 10 9 8 7 6
    ♥ A K Q J                           ♥ 10 9 8 7 6
    ♦ A K                               ♦ Q J
    ♣ K J 9 7                           ♣ —
                    SOUTH
                    ♠ 5 4 3 2
                    ♥ 5 4 3 2
                    ♦ —
                    ♣ 6 5 4 3 2
```

The Duke held the West hand in the diagram and incredible though it may appear, he never took a single trick.

Clubs were trumps and the Duke had the opening lead. In an effort to draw trumps as quickly as possible he led the seven of clubs. North

10

won with the eight and led a diamond which South ruffed. South returned a trump covered by the nine and ten. Another diamond ruff put South in again to lead his last trump. North won, drew the Duke's last trump and claimed the balance with his seven established diamond winners.

On this hand the Duke lost twenty thousand pounds, the equivalent today of over a million dollars. Of course the Duke was swindled. This hand was used by hustlers of the eighteenth and nineteenth centuries to take advantage of the betting habits of the day. The actual cards can be found in one of Hoyle's editions published long before the Duke's disaster.

From England, whist soon spread throughout most of Europe and the United States. No history of the game, however short, can fail to mention the famous French expert, Guillaume Deschapelles (1780-1847). He is described by his contemporary, James Clay, the English whist authority, as the finest whist player "beyond comparison the world has ever seen." Soldiering in one of the wars of the time he lost his right hand, severed at the wrist. Nevertheless he continued to play whist, chess, and more remarkably, billiards. Many bridge experts have been excellent chess players, and many chess experts have been excellent bridge players. But Deschapelles was acknowledged as the finest whist player and the finest chess player of his day.

Although he contributed much to the science of whist, Deschapelles is remembered chiefly as the inventor of the coup which bears his name. This is the deliberate sacrifice of a high unsupported honor in order to force an entry into partner's hand.

```
                      NORTH
                      ♠ —
                      ♥ A J
                      ♦ 6 5 4 3 2
                      ♣ K Q J 10 9 8
        WEST                             EAST
        ♠ 4 3 2                          ♠ Q 7 6 5
        ♥ Q 3 2                          ♥ K 7 6 5 4
        ♦ K Q J 10 9                     ♦ A
        ♣ 4 2                            ♣ 7 6 5
                      SOUTH
                      ♠ A K J 10 9 8
                      ♥ 10 9 8
                      ♦ 8 7
                      ♣ A 3
```

11

Against a contract of four spades West leads the diamond king to East's ace. What should East return at trick two?

The only return to beat the contract is the king of hearts, a Deschapelles coup. With any other return, West will never get in to cash his diamond winner. Try it.

The next great name to appear on the whist scene is that of Henry Jones (1831-1899) of London, better known by his pseudonym of "Cavendish." Author of many books on the game, he had more influence on whist than any writer since Hoyle. Among his contributions to the science of the game was the fourth-best lead, which has remained standard to this day. Cavendish devised and directed the first duplicate game, in London in 1857.

Toward the end of the nineteenth century, a variation of whist was introduced called "bridge." Instead of turning up the last card to determine trump, the dealer was allowed to chose the trump suit or notrump if he preferred. He also had the option of passing the decision to partner. Doubles and redoubles were permitted ad infinitum, introducing an undesirable gambling element. Another difference, and a crucial one, was that in bridge the dummy was exposed. This made the play more scientific and whist authorities actually recommended bridge to their pupils as an aid to improving their whist.

About 1904 the element of competitive bidding was introduced: All four players could now bid in turn as high as they wanted for the privilege of naming the trump suit. Called "auction bridge," this new variation quickly supplanted bridge, but the parent game, whist, continued to be played side by side with auction.

Further experiments, first by some English officers in India and then in France during World War I, produced a vital improvement: To score bonuses for games and slams you had to bid them. In 1925, on a cruise through the Panama Canal, Harold S. Vanderbilt combined this feature with a new scoring system including the idea of vulnerability and called it "contract bridge." Thanks to Vanderbilt's social position and tremendous reputation in the bridge world, contract bridge was immediately accepted and soon eclipsed all other forms of the game.

The credit for making contract bridge an international success must go to the dynamic Ely Culbertson (1891-1955). Expert player, author of an enormous number of bridge books, founder of *Bridge World* Magazine, and organizer of many bridge activities, Culbertson was the outstanding personality and world-wide authority in the early years of contract. Perhaps his greatest achievement was to persuade the public that it was socially unacceptable NOT to play bridge.

The World of Bridge Today

In 1937 various American organizations were united as the American Contract Bridge League. Today the A.C.B.L. has 180,000 members and sanctions 1200 tournaments a year throughout North America. The League has 4000 affiliated bridge clubs, providing duplicate games on a daily or weekly basis. Annual world championships are under the direction of the World Bridge Federation, which has a membership of 94 countries.

Tomorrow, when you sit down at the bridge table, remember that we are all part of this huge world of bridge. And just as the wonders of modern science are built on generations of research and experiment by scientists of yesterday, so the game of bridge today is a better game thanks to the cumulative contributions of the experts of the past.

What System Do You Play?

The vast majority of players in North America use Standard American bidding, derived from the ideas of Culbertson in the thirties and modified by Charles Goren in the fifties. Many bridge writers try to sell the reader a new system. Each assures him that if he adopts this new system he is bound to win more hands, more tournaments. I have no new bidding system to offer and I seriously doubt that a new system ever made a good bidder out of a bad one.

The way to improve your bridge is to cut down on your mistakes. A player who averages twenty errors in a session of bridge is twice as good as one who averages forty errors.

Naturally it is impossible to cut out all mistakes. Any player who averages less than two per session deserves the title of expert. (Of course in this rarefied atmosphere I am counting even such minute errors as the play of the three spot when the four would have been better.) The average player probably makes about one hundred errors in the bidding and play during an afternoon of bridge. Fortunately for his self-esteem, he will recognize only ten percent of them.

There are two main causes of error: bad judgment and ignorance. Errors in judgment are not easy to correct but errors due to ignorance are.

Standard American is basically a natural system of bidding. By natural I mean that if a player bids spades, he has spades. If he bids diamonds, he has diamonds, and so on. There are two important guide posts which distinguish one natural system from another: the forcing principles and the notrump structure. These two subjects will be discussed first.

2

Forcing Bids

It is hard to overemphasize the importance of forcing bids. They are as vital to bridge-players as traffic lights are to drivers of motor vehicles. If a driver does not know that red means "stop," green means "go" and amber means "caution," chaos and manslaughter can be the result.

So it is in bidding at the bridge table. The different kinds of forcing and non-forcing bids are the traffic signals of the auction. If partners are on different wavelengths here, chaos will often follow and attempted manslaughter must not be ruled out.

Many bidding disasters occur simply because a player does not know whether or not a certain bid is forcing. Most textbooks are prepared for beginners, and the author is obliged to concentrate on such problems as when or how to open the bidding, when to respond, and so on. If a reader wishes to review the subject of forcing bids, he will have trouble.

When the first edition of this book was written, more than 30 years ago, there was general agreement about what was and was not forcing. Since then there have been many changes. For example, strong two bids and strong jump overcalls are fast becoming extinct. Weak two bids and weak jump overcalls are here to stay and must be considered an integral part of Standard American.

Another change is the increase in the number of invitational bids. These strongly suggest game: Partner passes only with a bare minimum.

A bidding system is a language and like any other language it is continually in transition. This book recommends a style that is halfway between the traditional and the ultra-modern; a style that is easily adopted by the intermediate player without having to add too many artificial gadgets.

Forcing Principles

There are two kinds of forcing bids: Those which are forcing for one round only, and those which are forcing to game. If a bid is forcing to game, BOTH members of the partnership are obliged to continue bidding until game is reached or until the opposition has been doubled.

Principle #1. The only opening bid which is forcing is two clubs. This is artificial and has nothing to do with clubs. With very rare exceptions partner will respond two diamonds and opener now bids his suit or notrump as the case may be.

Example.

WEST	EAST
2♣	2♦
2♠	

West's bid of two spades shows an old-fashioned strong two-bid in spades. It is forcing and, unless otherwise agreed by the partnership, it is forcing to game on both players. (See chapter 8.)

Opening bids of two diamonds, two hearts and two spades are weak. They show a six-card suit and about 6-10 points. (See chapter 8.)

Principle #2. A new suit by responder is forcing for one round.

Example #1.

WEST	EAST
1♣	1♥

East may have only 6 points but he may have much more. His hand is virtually unlimited and West is obligated to give him another chance to bid.

Example #2.

WEST	EAST
1♣	1♥
2♣	2♦

East's bid of two diamonds is forcing, although not to game.

Exception.

WEST	EAST
1♣	1♠
1NT	2♥

16

When opener has rebid one notrump a new suit by responder is not forcing. Here East has a weak two-suiter which will not play well in notrump. He could hold:

♠ K 7 6 5 2   ♥ Q 9 8 6 2   ♦ 6   ♣ J 5

West is expected to correct to two spades with equal length in the majors or to pass if he prefers hearts.

Note: If responder is a passed hand, new suits by him are not forcing because his hand is limited.

Principle #3. A new suit response at the two-level is not only forcing, it promises another bid.

Example.	WEST	EAST
	1♥	2♣

For this bid at the two-level (referred to as two-over-one or 2/1), East needs ten or more high-card points. And he promises to bid at least once more.

Today, some play 2/1 as forcing to game unless responder immediately rebids his suit, and some play 2/1 unconditionally forcing to game. Unless you have such an agreement, however, assume that 2/1 promises another bid but is not game forcing.

Principle #4. A new suit by opener is not forcing.

Example:	WEST	EAST
	1♣	1♥
	1♠	

East may pass with a minimum such as:

♠ Q 7 6   ♥ K 7 6 3 2   ♦ 7 6 5   ♣ J 6

If West had a hand that was good enough to make a game opposite this, he would have rebid two spades not one spade.

Principle #5. A jump shift (a jump into a new suit) by either player is game forcing.

17

Example #1   WEST   EAST
               1♦   1♥
               2♠

Here opener's rebid of two spades is a jump shift and game-forcing. It shows a hand that expects to make game even if East has only six points.

Example #2.   WEST   EAST
               1♦   2♥

The jump shift by responder is not only game forcing, it strongly suggests a slam.

Principle #6. Other jump bids (below game) by either opener or responder are strong invitations but not forcing.

Example #1.   WEST   EAST   WEST   EAST
              1♠   3♠   or   1♦   3♦

These are both "limit raises" showing about 11 points. West will only pass with a minimum.

Example #2.   WEST   EAST
               1♦   1♠
               3♦

Opener's jump to three diamonds shows a long, strong diamond suit and a hand worth about 17 points. It is highly invitational but not forcing. East may pass with a minimum.

Example #3.   WEST   EAST
               1♣   1♥
               3♥

Opener's three-heart bid shows four-card heart support and a hand worth about 17 points. It is highly invitational but not forcing. With a slightly stronger hand he would rebid four hearts not three hearts.

Example #4.   WEST   EAST
               1♣   1♥
               1♠   2NT or 3♣ or 3♥ or 3♠

18

All these jump rebids by responder are strong invitations. (10-12 points.)

Note: In the traditional style described in the first edition of this book, jump bids by responder were forcing. This is out of fashion, although some players still play that way.

Principle #7. When a suit has been agreed upon, a new suit is forcing.

Example #1.	WEST	EAST
	1♠	2♠
	3♦	

East-West have agreed on spades. The three-diamond bid by West is a game try. He is hoping for help in the diamond suit. With no help East simply rebids three spades unless he has a maximum. With diamond help or a maximum East jumps to four spades or cue bids an ace. On no account may he pass three diamonds.

Principle #8. A bid by the opposition may relieve a player from his obligation to bid.

Example.	SOUTH	WEST	NORTH	EAST
	1♥	Pass	1♠	2♣
	?			

South can pass if he has nothing he wishes to say, because North will automatically get another chance to bid.

Principle #9. A reverse is forcing for one round.

Example.	WEST	EAST
	1♦	1♠
	2♥	

West's bid of two hearts is a reverse. He has bid his suits in reverse order (the lower-ranking before the higher-ranking) in such a way that partner cannot retreat to the first suit at the two-level. In this example, if East simply wants to give a preference to diamonds he has to go all the way to the three-level.

Note this sequence:

WEST	EAST
1♦	1♥
1♠	

Here the one-spade bid is not a reverse even though West has bid his suits in reverse order. The reason is that this time East can retreat to partner's first suit - diamonds - at the two-level.

It used to be that a reverse was highly invitational but not forcing. Today it is forcing for one round, but not to game.

Quiz on Forcing Bids

In the following sequences it is your turn to bid at the question mark. If you could possibly pass put a check mark in the column headed NF for nonforcing. If you are obliged to make another bid put a check mark in the column headed F for forcing. And if both you and partner must continue bidding until game is reached put a check mark in the column headed GF for game forcing.

	WEST	EAST	NF	F	GF
1.	1♣	?	—	—	—
2.	1♣	1♦			
	1♥	1♠			
	?		—	—	—
3.	1♥	1♠			
	3♠	?	—	—	—
4.	1♦	1♥			
	2♦	2NT			
	?		—	—	—

20

5. WEST   EAST
    3♦   3♥
    ?   –   –   –

6. WEST   EAST
    1♦   1♥
    2♣   ?   –   –   –

7. WEST   EAST
    1♥   2♥
    3♣   ?   –   –   –

8. WEST   EAST
    1♣   1♥
    2♠   ?   –   –   –

9. WEST   EAST
    1♦   2NT
    ?   –   –   –

10. WEST   EAST
    1♦   1♠
    2♣   3♦

21

Answers to Quiz

1. NF. The only forcing opening bid is two clubs.

2. F. A new suit by responder is forcing for one round.

3. NF. Jumps are invitational, not forcing, except in a new suit.

4. NF. Two notrump invites game, showing about 11 points.

5. F. New suits by responder are forcing.

6. NF. New suits by opener are not forcing.

7. F. When a suit has been agreed, a new suit is forcing.

8. GF. A jump shift is forcing to game.

9. NF. This is highly invitational but not forcing.

10. NF. Again, this is highly invitational but not forcing.

Rate Yourself as Follows:

No mistakes .... Expert!
One or two mistakes..................... Very good.
Three or four mistakes .... Above average
Five or six mistakes .... Average.
Seven or more mistakes................ Why not just reread the chapter
　　　　　　　　　　　　　　　　　　and try the quiz again.

3

The Notrump Structure

The backbone of any bidding system is its notrump structure. In order to determine how many tricks you and partner can take at notrump, a point-count method of evaluating honors is useful. The one devised by Milton Work and made popular by Charles Goren is universally used today because it is so simple.

> An ace counts *4 points.*
> A king counts *3 points.*
> A queen counts *2 points.*
> A jack counts *1 point.*

There are thus 40 points in the deck, and an average hand will have 10.

37 points between your hand and partner's should produce thirteen tricks at notrump. For example: four aces, four kings, four queens and one jack make thirteen tricks. This is not a guarantee, but the odds are greatly in your favor. And with 37 out of a possible 40 points, you cannot be missing an ace so Blackwood is not needed.

Similarly 33 points in the combined hands should produce six notrump. Again you cannot be missing two aces so you do not need Blackwood.

26 points in the combined hands should produce the nine tricks needed for game in notrump.

> Seven notrump: 37 points
> Six notrump: 33 points
> Three notrump: 26 points

Notrump Distribution

To open one notrump you will normally have one of these distributions:

4-3-3-3
4-4-3-2
5-3-3-2

With a five-card major suit and 5-3-3-2 distribution, you have a choice. Some experts never open one notrump with a five-card major. Others frequently do. Take your pick.

The point-count required to open one notrump is slightly lower than it used to be. (15-17 rather than 16-18). This reflects the fact that modern bidders tend to open with many 12-point hands rather than wait for 13.

Some players are afraid to open one notrump holding a weak doubleton. This is false economy. Suppose you open one diamond holding:

♠ 3 2   ♥ A J 10   ♦ K Q J 8   ♣ A J 4 3

Partner will probably respond one spade. Now you cannot rebid one notrump because that would show a balanced 12-14. And you cannot jump to two notrump because that would show a balanced 18-19. True, you can rebid two clubs but that certainly does not show a balanced hand and it does not show 15-17. The only way to show a balanced 15-17 is to open one notrump in the first place.

Moral: With the right point-count and the right shape, do not fool around. Open one notrump.

The Entire Notrump Structure At a Glance

Open one of a suit and
rebid one notrump 12-14

Open one notrump 15-17

Open one of a suit and
jump in notrump 18-19

24

(Some players assign slightly different values to the higher ranges.)

You do not need to memorize these ranges. Just remember that one notrump is 15-17. And notice that the ranges are all very narrow except for the first two where you bid one notrump either immediately or as a rebid. In these two cases partner can always bid two notrump to invite game. All the higher ranges need to be very narrow because there is no room for partner to invite game.

Responding to One Notrump With a Balanced Hand

Any time partner bids any number of notrump you become the captain. If you are balanced, usually all you have to do is add your points to his and place the contract, keeping in mind those three milestones:

> 37 points *are needed for a grand slam.*
> 33 points *are needed for a small slam.*
> 26 points *are needed for game.*

In a pinch, 25 points will do for three notrump if the points are fairly evenly divided between declarer and dummy. Thus 15 opposite 10 is acceptable, but 23 opposite 2 will probably fail due to lack of entries to dummy. Intermediate cards often spell the difference between "good" and "bad" holdings: A 10 9 8 is much better than A 7 4 2. And count a 5-card suit as a point.

Therefore when partner opens one notrump:

> With 0 to a bad 8 .... Pass
>
> With 9 (or a good 8) 2NT
>
> With 10-15 .... 3NT

With 16-17 .... 4NT
(Not Blackwood. It invites 6NT.)

With 18-19 .... 6NT

With 20-21 .... 5NT
(Forcing, invites 7NT)

With 22-25 .... 7NT

Do not memorize these responses. Simply add your points to partner's known 15-17 and use your head.

Responding to Two Notrump When You Are Balanced

Again, add your points to partner's known 20-21 and act accordingly.

With 0-4 .... Pass

With 5-11 .... 3NT

With 12 .... 4NT
(Not Blackwood. This invites 6NT.)

With 13-15 .... 6NT

With 16 .... 5NT
(Forcing, invites 7NT)

With 17-20 .... 7NT

The Double-Cross

Notice that when a player is the first to bid notrump his partner becomes temporary captain because he has an exact picture of the partnership assets. An auction such as the following just does not exist.

WEST	EAST
1♦	1♥
2NT	3NT
6NT!	

This is a double-cross. When West bids two notrump, East becomes

26

captain. He knows his partner has a balanced 18-19. He adds his points to this and determines that game in notrump is feasible. West should have his mouth washed out with soap for that ridiculous bid of six notrump.

The Stayman Convention

As a general rule, when you and your partner together hold eight cards or more in a major suit, it is easier to make game in that suit than in notrump. The ruffing power is usually worth a trick or two. Furthermore the fact that your side has an eight-card fit in one suit increases the chances that another suit will be inadequately stopped at notrump.

When partner opens one notrump and you have one or two four-card major suits, you need to be able to locate a four-four major fit if you are interested in game. The way to do this is to make an artificial response of two clubs. This is the Stayman convention and it asks opener to bid a major suit if he can. It has nothing to do with clubs.

Opener's Rebids:

2♥ shows four hearts.
2♠ shows four spades.
2♦ denies a four-card major. It has nothing to do with diamonds.

With both four-card majors most people bid hearts first but this is not important.

Example 1:

WEST	EAST
♠ K J 4	♠ Q 10 3 2
♥ K 10 9 2	♥ Q J 4 3
♦ A 2	♦ 10 4 3
♣ A J 3 2	♣ K Q

WEST	EAST
1NT	2♣
2♥	4♥

Four hearts is a good contract. Three notrump, likely without Stayman, is terrible.
Switch the red suits in the West hand and the bidding will be:

```
WEST              EAST
1NT               2♣
2♦                3NT
```

This time East knows that there is no eight-card major-suit fit and he bids three notrump which is an excellent contract.

Example 2:
```
WEST              EAST
♠ K 10 6 5        ♠ A Q 4 2
♥ A K 7 2         ♥ 6 4
♦ Q J             ♦ K 8
♣ K J 10          ♣ Q 9 7 6 4

WEST              EAST
1NT               2♣
2♥                3NT
4♠
```

East's bidding implies four spades, since with no major suit he would have bid three notrump directly. So West can safely bid four spades. Notice that four spades will probably make an overtrick but three notrump is bound to fail if the opening leader produces a diamond.

If responder is slightly weaker, he bids more gently at his second turn:

Example 3:   ♠ K 4 3 2   ♥ Q 4 3 2   ♦ J   ♣ K 8 6 2

You still bid two clubs in response to partner's opening one notrump. But if partner shows a four-card major you will raise only to the three-level, leaving partner to go to game with a maximum or pass with a minimum. If the rebid is two diamonds, you bid only two notrump. Again opener will decide whether to continue, based on the strength of his hand.

Normally you need about eight points to use Stayman. But occasionally you will be able to use it with a very bad hand, SHORT IN CLUBS.

Example 4:   ♠ J 8 5 3   ♥ J 7 3   ♦ 9 8 6 3 2   ♣ 2

Partner opens one notrump which you can see is a hopeless contract.

Here you can use Stayman to find a better spot. If partner shows a four- card major, leave him to play there. And if he denies a four-card major by bidding two diamonds, leave him there.

Over an opening bid of two notrump, three clubs by partner is Stayman. Similarly if the auction proceeds:

WEST	EAST
2♣	2♦
2NT	3♣

Again three clubs is Stayman asking for a four-card major. The only difference is that West is known to have 22-23 points this time.

Quiz on Notrump Bidding

You are the dealer. What do you bid with the following?

1. ♠ A Q 4   ♥ A Q 5 3   ♦ 7 5   ♣ A 8 6 4

2. ♠ A J 7   ♥ A J 10   ♦ A Q 6   ♣ A J 9 8

3. ♠ K Q 6   ♥ Q 6 4   ♦ K J 8   ♣ Q J 9 5

4. ♠ A Q 7   ♥ Q J 8   ♦ A 7 5   ♣ A Q 6 4

5. ♠ A Q J   ♥ A Q 8 7   ♦ A Q 7   ♣ A 10 9

Partner opens one notrump. What do you bid with the following?

6. ♠ K 6 4   ♥ K 8 6   ♦ Q 6 4 2   ♣ 9 7 4

7. ♠ J 7   ♥ A K Q   ♦ A Q J 9   ♣ K Q J 2

8. ♠ A Q 3 2   ♥ A Q 6   ♦ 7 6 5 2   ♣ 8 6

Partner opens one diamond, you respond one heart and partner rebids one notrump. What do you do now with this?

9. ♠ K 9 8   ♥ A Q 8 2   ♦ 8 6 5   ♣ Q J 8

Answers to Quiz on Notrump Bidding

1. Open one notrump to show a balanced 15-17.

2. Open two notrump to show a balanced 20-21.

3. Open one club planning to rebid one notrump. Notice that it takes two bids to describe a balanced 12-14.

4. You are too strong for one notrump and not strong enough for two notrump. Open one club, then over partner's response you will jump to two notrump to show a balanced 18-19.

5. You are too strong to open two notrump. Open two clubs, (artificial and forcing.) Partner will probably bid two diamonds and you will rebid two notrump showing a balanced 22-23. Partner now becomes captain and can usually place the final contract. He can also pass if he has nothing.

6. You have a very bad 8 points. Pass.

7. Your side has 38-40 points. Bid seven notrump.

8. Bid two clubs (Stayman). Over two spades bid four spades. Otherwise bid three notrump.

9. Bid two notrump inviting game.

Rate Yourself as Follows:

No mistakes .... Expert.
1-2 mistakes .... Good.
3-6 mistakes .... Average.
7-9 mistakes .... Well at least you are honest.

4

Responding to Notrump with an Unbalanced Hand

Suppose partner opens one notrump and you hold the following:

Hand #1.   ♠ 9 8 2   ♥ J 8 6 4 3 2   ♦ 10 6 5   ♣ 7

This hand will play much better in hearts than notrump. Thirty years ago you would have bid two hearts which was known as a "drop dead" bid. It showed a bad hand with at least five hearts and partner was expected to pass.

If you had a good hand with at least five hearts you would have jumped in your suit.

Hand #2.   ♠ K J 5   ♥ A Q 6 4 3   ♦ 7 6 2   ♣ J 3

This time you would bid three hearts in response to the one notrump. With an eight-card major-suit fit it is better to play four of a major than three notrump. So partner was expected to raise to four hearts if he had three (or more). With only two-card support he would rebid three notrump.

Many people still play this way, but the majority of experienced players today use a convention invented by Oswald Jacoby, known as Jacoby Transfer Bids.

Jacoby Transfer Bids Over One Notrump

A response of two diamonds shows five or more hearts and requires opener to bid two hearts.

31

A response of two hearts shows five or more spades and requires opener to bid two spades.

There are substantial advantages to these transfers. First let us see how they work in the above examples.

With hand #1 you respond two diamonds. Partner is required to bid two hearts and you pass. Notice that it is much better for partner to be declarer so the opening lead will come up to the strong hand.

With hand #2 the auction will be:

PARTNER	YOU
1NT	2♦
2♥	3NT
4♥ or pass	

Your first move is to bid two diamonds, a transfer, and partner obediently bids two hearts. Now you jump to three notrump. This shows game values and exactly five hearts. (If you had the same hand with six hearts you would know the partnership had at least eight hearts and your second bid would be four hearts, not three notrump.) Over your three notrump partner bids four hearts, unless he has only a doubleton heart in which case he passes. Notice that whether the final contract is three notrump or four hearts, the stronger hand gets to be declarer.

The Jacoby transfer bid works particularly well with invitational hands.

Hand #3   ♠ K J 8 6 5   ♥ A 4   ♦ 9 6 2   ♣ 7 5 4

PARTNER	YOU
1NT	2♥
2♠	2NT
?	

Partner opens one notrump and your first move is to bid two hearts, a transfer showing at least five spades. Partner obediently bids two spades. Now you bid two notrump. This is the equivalent of bidding two notrump over the opening one notrump except that it also promises exactly five spades. Partner has four choices: With a minimum and only two spades he passes. With a minimum and three trumps for you he bids three spades and you pass. With a maximum and only two spades he bids three notrump. And with a maximum and three spades he jumps to four spades.

After responder transfers, new suits by him are forcing.

Hand #4	PARTNER	YOU
	♠ Q J 8	♠ A K 9 8 6
	♥ A J 9 6	♥ Q 7
	♦ A 8 6	♦ 7
	♣ K J 2	♣ A Q 10 6 5

PARTNER	YOU
1NT	2♥
2♠	3♣
4♠	4NT
5♥	6♠

Your bid of three clubs is forcing and partner revalues his hand. He not only has three spades for you, they are GOOD spades. In addition, he has two helpful honors in your second suit. And aces are always welcome. He jumps to four spades and you are happy to carry on to slam.

What about minor suits? This is a complex area, and the modern expert style is described in Chapter 11.

In the original Jacoby transfer method, a response of two spades showed length in both minor suits and many use that today.

I suggest that, for a time, you use a method now popular because it is featured on the "Yellow Card" — the basic system used by players on the Internet.

Use two spades to show a weak hand with a long minor suit, at least six cards. Partner is required to bid three clubs. If you have clubs you pass. If you have diamonds you bid three diamonds and partner passes.

When you have an invitational hand with a long minor you can jump to three clubs or three diamonds immediately. Suppose you hold:

Hand #5   ♠ J 7   ♥ 9 8   ♦ K Q 10 8 6 4   ♣ 8 7 5

PARTNER	YOU
1NT	3♦
?	

Over partner's notrump you jump to three diamonds. Partner will pass with a poor diamond holding. He will bid three notrump with a good diamond holding.

Hand #6   ♠ A 9 8   ♥ A K 2   ♦ A 3 2   ♣ J 9 3 2

With this hand partner can expect to make six diamond tricks plus two hearts and a spade, so he bids three notrump.

Hand #7   ♠ A 9 8   ♥ A K J 2   ♦ 7 5   ♣ A J 4 2

This time partner's diamond holding is hopeless for notrump so he passes three diamonds.
  When you have a slammish hand with a minor you can use Stayman and then bid your minor.

Hand #8

PARTNER	YOU
♠ K Q 9 8	♠ 9
♥ K Q 7	♥ A 5 4
♦ 7 4	♦ A Q 9 8 5 2
♣ A Q 4 2	♣ K J 9

PARTNER	YOU
1NT	2♣
2♠	3♦
3NT	Pass

Your three-diamond bid is now forcing. It is a way of suggesting a slam in diamonds and does not necessarily show a major. If partner had a suitable hand, six diamonds would be excellent. As it is, however, partner's diamonds are dreadful and he rejects the idea by returning to notrump. You do not have enough to continue in the face of this rejection.

Note: Transfers are off in competition.

SOUTH	WEST	NORTH	EAST
1NT	2♦	2♥	

North's two-heart bid is NOT a transfer to spades. It is a "drop dead" bid in hearts. How else can North-South get to play two hearts?

TIP: With 5-4 (or 4-5) in the majors and an invitational hand or better, it is usually preferable to use Stayman rather than to transfer.

You hold: ♠ K J 8 7 5   ♥ K J 7 6   ♦ 5 4   ♣ 6 3

Over partner's one notrump, bid two clubs. If partner shows a major you are in good shape. If he denies a major, you will rebid two spades, showing five spades and invitational values.

WARNING: Responder holds:

♠ K Q 9 8 2   ♥ K 9 8   ♦ K 5   ♣ 10 9 7

OPENER	RESPONDER
1NT	2♥
2♠	?

Players who have just adopted transfers tend to say to themselves at this point, "Wow! Partner bid spades. Look at the great support I have for him." And they jump to four spades without thinking.

Try to remember that partner did not bid spades. You forced him to open his mouth and say two spades. You must bid three notrump now. Partner knows you have five spades and he will only pass three notrump if he has a doubleton spade.

Quiz on Transfer Bids

Partner opens one notrump. What is your plan with the following hands?

1. ♠ Q 7 5 3 2 ♥ 7 ♦ 9 7 4 3 ♣ 10 8 6

2. ♠ A Q 9 7 6 ♥ K 8 ♦ Q 7 5 2 ♣ J 8

3. ♠ 7 6 ♥ K Q 8 7 6 ♦ K 10 9 ♣ 10 6 5

4. ♠ Q J 9 8 6 4 ♥ 8 ♦ A Q 6 4 ♣ 9 8

5. ♠ K J 8 6 5 2 ♥ 8 ♦ K 8 6 5 ♣ 7 5

6. ♠ 9 8 ♥ 3 2 ♦ A K Q J 8 6 ♣ 7 6 4

7. ♠ 8 ♥ 8 6 2 ♦ J 7 5 ♣ A Q 9 7 5 2

8. ♠ 8 ♥ 8 6 2 ♦ J 8 7 6 4 2 ♣ 7 5 2

Partner opens two notrump. What do you do?

9. ♠ 5 ♥ 9 5 4 3 2 ♦ 6 4 3 2 ♣ 9 4 2

10. ♠ A Q 7 5 3 ♥ J 8 ♦ 6 4 2 ♣ 7 5 3

Answers to Quiz on Transfer Bids

1. Bid two hearts (transfer) and plan to pass partner in two spades.

2. Again you transfer to spades. This time you follow up with three notrump. Partner will continue to four spades unless he has only a doubleton spade, in which case he will pass three notrump.

3. You bid two diamonds (transfer) and when partner obediently bids two hearts you bid two notrump showing five hearts and invitational values.

4. Bid two hearts and when partner bids two spades you will jump to four spades.

36

5. Again you transfer to spades, but this time you only invite game by bidding three spades next.

6. Bid three notrump. You will provide six tricks and partner should be able to muster up at least three. There is no reason to mention the diamond suit.

7. Bid three clubs, invitational. Partner will pass with a poor club holding and he will bid three notrump with a good club holding.

8. Bid two spades. This shows a weak hand with a long minor. Partner bids three clubs, and you bid three diamonds. He passes.

9. Bid three diamonds forcing partner to bid three hearts, then pass. He may not make it. But he has a better chance at three hearts than he does at two notrump.

10. Bid three hearts, transferring to spades, then bid three notrump.

Rate Yourself as Follows:

No mistakes .... Expert.

1-2 mistakes .... Good

3-6 mistakes .... Average

7-9 mistakes .... Have you considered taking up gin rummy?

5

The Opening One-Bid

Most players know that a hand worth 13 points qualifies as an opening bid but they may not know where the number 13 comes from. The answer is this: It has been determined that about 26 points are needed to make a game. If both partners pass with 13 points each they may easily pass out a game. It is logical, therefore, than any hand worth 13 or more should be opened.

How to Evaluate Unbalanced Hands

While the 4-3-2-1 point count is very satisfactory for notrump bidding, it is not adequate for bidding unbalanced hands. Several methods have been devised for translating distributional values into point count. The simplest is the asset system:

Asset Points for Distribution

> A singleton counts as one asset.

> A void counts as two assets.

> A long suit counts as one asset.

> An asset is the equivalent of one point.

Assets become very significant as the bidding develops, and may boom or slump depending on the degree of fit established. An eight-card trump fit is normal and if you find such a fit the value of your assets does not change.

No eight-card fit: Assets slump to zero.

Eight-card fit: Assets unchanged.

Nine-card fit: Assets double.

Ten-card fit: Assets triple.

And so on.

(Note: If you are considering bidding notrump at some point, a long suit is still an asset but a void or singleton is not.)

Example #1. As dealer you hold:

♠ A Q 9 4 2   ♥ A 10 7 6 4   ♦ 5 3   ♣ 6

This hand is worth 13 points.(10 points in high cards, plus three assets, one for each long suit and one for the singleton.) Bid one spade.

Example #2. Partner deals and opens one heart and next hand passes. You hold:

♠ 7 5   ♥ A 9 7 5 3   ♦ 9 8 6 5 2   ♣ 8

Your assets zoomed when partner bid one heart. He must have five so you are sure of a ten-card fit and your original three assets have tripled to nine. Counting the ace your hand is now worth thirteen and you should jump to four hearts. Suppose partner has a minimum such as:

♠ A 8 6   ♥ K 8 6 4 2   ♦ A 7   ♣ J 6 4

He figures to lose only three tricks and four hearts is where you belong.

Unguarded Honors

An unguarded honor is a defect. For example, a singleton king may be no better than a deuce if an opponent leads the ace. In such cases count the singleton either as an asset or as a king but do not count both.

39

Judgment

When the value of your hand comes to about 13 points it is necessary to use a little judgment to decide whether to open. A good general rule is this: Always open a hand worth 14. Usually open a hand worth 13. Sometimes open a hand worth 12. Base your decision on these judgment factors.

Judgment Factor #1. Good Points vs. Bad Points

In the 4-3-2-1 point count, the ace and king are undervalued in comparison with the lower honors, and the useful ten is not counted at all. Although queens and jacks pull their weight at a notrump contract, they are sometimes useless in a suit contract. Consequently, when you bid a suit you should eye with favor a hand with good points, (aces and kings) and discount slightly a hand with bad points (queens and jacks).

Judgment Factor #2. Quick Tricks

$$A = 1 \text{ quick trick.}$$
$$AK = 2 \text{ quick tricks.}$$
$$AQ = 1^1/_2 \text{ quick tricks.}$$
$$KQ = 1 \text{ quick trick.}$$
$$Kx = {}^1/_2 \text{ quick trick.}$$
$$QJx = {}^1/_2 \text{ quick trick.}$$

An opening bid usually contains about $2^1/_2$ quick tricks. You should rarely pass a hand with three or more quick tricks and you should rarely open a hand with less than two quick tricks.

Judgment Factor #3: Combination of Honor Cards

A combination of honors is more valuable than honors which are separated.

Hand A: ♠ A Q J 10   ♥ 4 3 2   ♦ 6 5 2   ♣ 5 3 2

Hand B: ♠ A 5 4 2   ♥ Q 3 2   ♦ J 4 2   ♣ 10 5 4

Hand A is worth more than hand B.

Judgment Factor #4: The Location of Honors

Honors are more valuable if they are located in your long suits.

Hand A: ♠ A K 10 8 4 2   ♥ K J 8 5   ♦ 2   ♣ 6 5

Hand B: ♠ 10 8 6 5 4 2   ♥ J 8 5 2   ♦ K   ♣ A K

Hand A is a clear-cut opening bid. Hand B is borderline.

Bidding a Major Suit

When you open one heart or one spade, partner will expect you to hold five or more cards in the suit and a hand worth 13-20 points.

Example #1. ♠ A 6   ♥ 10 8 6 4 2   ♦ A 3 2   ♣ A 7 5

Open one heart. Three quick tricks are not to be sneezed at.

Example #2. ♠ K J 7   ♥ A K J 8 7 5   ♦ Q J 2   ♣ K

Open one heart. This is a lot better than the hand in example #1 but there will be no game if partner cannot respond.

Bidding a Minor Suit

When you open one club or one diamond, you normally hold four or more cards in the suit and a hand worth 13-20.

Example #1. ♠ A K J 6   ♥ K 7   ♦ 6 5 3   ♣ Q 8 5 2

Open one club.   -

Example #2. ♠ A 8 7   ♥ Q 6   ♦ K Q   ♣ A Q J 7 4 3

Open one club.

Telling a White Lie

Occasionally you will get an opening bid with no five-card major and no four-card minor. If the point count is not suitable for notrump, you will have to tell a little white lie. And the whitest of these is to open a three-card minor.

Example #1. ♠ K 8 5 3   ♥ Q 5 4   ♦ A J 8   ♣ A 7 5

Open one club. When forced to choose between two three-card minors, bid one club.

Example #2. ♠ A 6 4 2   ♥ K 8 6 5   ♦ A Q 8   ♣ 8 7

Bid one diamond. Do not open a doubleton.

Which Suit Should You Bid First?

Holding a two-suited hand the general rule is this: With two suits of unequal length, bid the longer one first. With two suits of equal length, bid the higher-ranking one first.

Example #1. ♠ 7 4   ♥ 8   ♦ A K 7 5 2   ♣ A Q 8 7 5

Open one diamond, the higher-ranking of two equal suits. Then plan to bid clubs twice if given the chance. Partner will realize you have at least five clubs (you bid them twice) and at least five diamonds (you bid them first.) He now knows ten of your cards.

Example #2. ♠ A Q 9 8 6   ♥ 7   ♦ A K J 8 6 4   ♣ 4

Open one diamond, your longest suit. Next round bid spades and the next round rebid the spades. The auction might start like this:

YOU	PARTNER
1♦	1♥
1♠	2♣
2♠	

At this point partner will know you have five spades (because you bid them twice) and at least six diamonds (the diamond suit must be longer than the spades or you would not have bid it first.) This time partner knows eleven of your cards already and the auction is still at the two level!

EXCEPTION: With two ADJACENT long suits and a MINIMUM, it is often better to bid the higher-ranking suit first even if the lower-ranking suit is slightly longer.

Example: ♠ 6 ♥ A Q 9 8 6 ♦ K Q 6 4 3 2 ♣ 6

Open one heart. If you open one diamond here, partner will probably respond one spade. Now if you bid two hearts you will have reversed showing a very powerful hand which you do not have. With a minimum it is better to pretend your two suits are of equal length. Open one heart, then bid and rebid the diamonds showing at least 5-5.

Third-Seat Opening Bids

In third position a "shaded" opening with about a queen less than normal is possible. The reason is that your partner is a passed hand and his response therefore will not be forcing. If your opening bid was shaded you will simply pass his response and play for a partial. In third seat if you are opening with less than full values consider a good four-card major.

WEST	NORTH	EAST	SOUTH
Pass	Pass	?	

What should East bid with the following?

♠ Q 4 3 ♥ A K Q 9 ♦ 10 8 5 ♣ 8 7 2

Open one heart. You plan to pass whatever partner says. If South becomes declarer you want West to lead a heart. The five-card major restriction applies only to first- and second-hand opening bids.

Fourth-Seat Opening Bids

A fourth-seat opening bid promises about the same strength as one in first or second seat. There is, however, no need to prepare for a rebid since partner is a passed hand. If you have length in spades you will find it advantageous to open slightly under strength. Similarly if you are short in spades, you should be wary of opening a minimum. The reason is that when you are contemplating passing out a hand in fourth position, it means that the high cards are fairly evenly distributed around the table. Both sides can probably make a part-score in their longest suit. The side with spades has a tremendous advantage in any part-score battle.

Quiz on Opening Bids

You are the dealer. What is your plan for each of the following hands?

1. ♠ A Q 10 6 5   ♥ A J 9 8   ♦ 4 3 2   ♣ 7

2. ♠ K Q 6   ♥ Q J 2   ♦ Q 7 6 5   ♣ Q 9 6

3. ♠ A Q 5   ♥ K J 8   ♦ K Q 10 9 8   ♣ 8 7

4. ♠ A J 10 8 7   ♥ 5 4   ♦ —   ♣ A K 8 7 5 4

5. ♠ A K 9 8   ♥ A 9 7 2   ♦ J 9 8   ♣ 9 7

6. ♠ K Q 10 7 2   ♥ K Q 7 6 4 2   ♦ Q   ♣ 8

Answers to Quiz

1. Open one spade. You will probably bid two hearts next depending on partner's response.

2. Pass. But plan to be aggressive if partner opens the bidding.

3. Open one notrump and leave the rest to partner. This is easy.

4. Open one club and if given the chance you will bid spades twice on the next two rounds. Partner will assume you have five spades and longer clubs.

5. Open one diamond. Partner will probably bid one heart or one spade and you plan to raise him to the two-level next round.

6. Open one spade. With two adjacent long suits and a minimum, treat the suits as equal and bid the higher-ranking first. You are not strong enough to reverse.

6

Responses to Opening Bids
of One in a Suit

When partner opens the bidding he launches your side on a search for game. Suppose he bids one heart. You can assume he has five or more hearts and a hand worth 13-20 points. It takes about 26 points to make a game. If you have less than six points you should pass. Game is remote.

Partner opens one heart and you hold:

1. ♠ Q 9 6 3   ♥ 7 3   ♦ J 6 2   ♣ J 7 4 2

2. ♠ K Q 7 5   ♥ J 8   ♦ 8 7 6 2   ♣ 8 6 5

3. ♠ K Q 8 6 5   ♥ J 8   ♦ A Q 6 2   ♣ A 8

Pass with hand #1. If you bid you will probably get overboard.

On hands #2 and #3 bid one spade. This simply shows four or more spades and six or more points. For further details partner will have to wait until next round.

Raising Partner

The most helpful response is the direct raise, particularly of partner's major suit. When evaluating your hand for a raise count your assets and make the necessary adjustments. Remember that they double with a nine-card fit, triple with a ten card fit, and so on.

You assume an eight-card fit if you have three cards in partner's major.

The Single Raise (6-9)

PARTNER	YOU
1♥	2♥

With the equivalent of 6-9 points, (occasionally a bad 10), and at least three cards in partner's major, give him a single raise.

You could hold:

1. ♠ 6   ♥ K 8 5 3   ♦ Q 10 8 5   ♣ 9 8 3 2

2. ♠ J 7   ♥ A 9 5   ♦ 10 8 7 3 2   ♣ K 9 7

3. ♠ Q 7 6 4 2   ♥ K 8 6 2   ♦ 8 2   ♣ 9 7

With each of these hands it is right to raise partner to two hearts. Some might bid one spade on #3, but the hand is worth only one bid and your first duty is to support partner's major if possible.

Raising Partner's Minor

The requirements for a single raise of partner's minor are slightly different because he has not shown a five-card suit and might have only a three-card suit. You usually have five trumps to raise him and you still need a hand worth 6-9 points.

However, it is so important to locate the eight-card MAJOR suit fit that you should not raise the minor if you can bid a major yourself.

(Remember that it takes eleven tricks to make a game in a minor and only ten in a major. For this reason all bidding systems are geared to locating the major-suit fit if one exists.)

Partner opens one diamond. You hold:

♠ K 6 2   ♥ 8 7   ♦ K J 7 5 2   ♣ 9 8 7

Bid two diamonds. You show a hand worth 6-9, with probably five diamonds and no four-card major.

You hold: ♠ Q 8 5 2   ♥ 8 7   ♦ A J 5 3 2   ♣ 9 8

Bid one spade. It is all important to locate the eight-card major-suit fit if one exists.

The Limit Raise (10-12)

PARTNER	YOU
1♠	3♠

You hold: ♠ K J 8 6   ♥ A 6   ♦ K 3 2   ♣ 9 7 5 2

You and partner have agreed to play the modern style where all jumps by responder are invitational. With four trumps and 10-12 points, jump to three spades. This is highly invitational but not forcing. It is called a "limit raise." If partner has a dead minimum he will pass. With a little extra he will carry on to game.

The Double Raise of a Minor

The limit raise of a minor usually shows five-card support and a hand worth 10-12. Again you should not raise the minor immediately if you can bid a major suit first. (Four of a major is the most desirable game if you have at least eight trumps. If you have no eight-card major-suit fit, three notrump is the second choice, providing there is no obvious weak suit. Bidding five of a minor is the third choice.)

Partner deals and bids one diamond. You hold:

♠ K J 8   ♥ 7 6   ♦ A Q J 3 2   ♣ 9 8 2

Respond three diamonds. But if you hold:

♠ K J 8 5   ♥ 6 5   ♦ A Q 6 3 2   ♣ J 8

Respond one spade and jump in diamonds next time.

The Triple Raise of Partner's Major

PARTNER	YOU
1♥	4♥

You hold: ♠ 6   ♥ Q 9 8 6 2   ♦ A 10 9 8 2   ♣ 8 6

Your four-heart bid usually shows five trumps and not more than nine high-card points. It is known as a "shut-out" bid because it is an effort to shut the enemy out of the auction. Furthermore, with a ten-card fit

47

you figure to make four hearts. Notice that you have almost no defense against four spades.

What About Stronger Raises? (13-15)

You hold: ♠ J 9 8 2   ♥ A K 2   ♦ 3 2   ♣ A Q 8 4

PARTNER	YOU
1 ♠	2 ♣
2 ♦	4 ♠

You know there is a game, so you must be careful not to make a bid which could be passed. An immediate jump to four spades might result in missing a slam. Partner would think you held a "shut-out" bid. One solution is to bid a new suit first, then jump to game in partner's major next round.

Note: A more accurate way to make a forcing raise in a major is described in Chapter 11.

Notrump Responses to Bids of One of a Suit

The Response of One Notrump (6-9)

You hold: ♠ K J 8   ♥ 8 7   ♦ 9 8 2   ♣ K 9 7 5 2

PARTNER	YOU
1 ♦	1NT

With 6-9 points (occasionally a bad 10), and with no four-card major that can be bid at the one level, respond one notrump. In this case you are almost sure to have club length, because you were unable to bid a major suit or raise diamonds.

But if you hold:

♠ K J   ♥ J 7 5 2   ♦ 9 7 6   ♣ K 9 7 4

You must bid one heart. The first priority is to locate a possible eight-card major suit fit. Do not bypass a four-card major to bid one notrump.

A Response of Two Notrump to a Minor (10-12)

You hold: ♠ K Q 8   ♥ Q J 6   ♦ Q 9 8   ♣ J 9 7 6

PARTNER	YOU
1♦	2NT

Again you deny a four-card major. This time you promise a balanced hand and should have stoppers in both major suits. In the modern style this jump is highly invitational, but not forcing. You should have 10-12 high-card points.

A Response of Three Notrump to a Minor (13-15)

You hold: ♠ K Q 7   ♥ A Q 8   ♦ J 9 6   ♣ Q 9 8 7

PARTNER	YOU
1♦	3NT

With a balanced 13-15, no four-card major, and all unbid suits stopped, jump to three notrump.

Note: A response of two notrump to a major is specialized and will be discussed in Chapter 11. A jump to three notrump over partner's major is a balanced 13-15 just as it is over a minor.

Bidding a New Suit

Responder may bid a new suit at the one-level with six or more high-card points. To bid a new suit at the two-level requires ten or more high-card points.

Partner opens one diamond. You hold:

♠ J 8 4 2   ♥ 9 8   ♦ J 9 8   ♣ A 9 6 2

Bid one spade.

Partner opens one heart. You hold:

♠ A K 6   ♥ 8 6   ♦ 7 4 3   ♣ K J 10 8 6

Bid two clubs.

49

Again partner opens one heart. This time you hold:

$$\spadesuit \text{K J 4} \quad \heartsuit \text{8 6} \quad \diamondsuit \text{7 4 3} \quad \clubsuit \text{K J 10 8 6}$$

Bid one notrump. You are not strong enough to bid at the two level.

Which Suit Should Responder Bid First?

With two suits of unequal length the general rule is to bid the longer suit first.

Partner opens one heart. You hold:

$$\spadesuit \text{A K J 8} \quad \heartsuit \text{7} \quad \diamondsuit \text{A Q 7 4 2} \quad \clubsuit \text{J 8 5}$$

Bid two diamonds. Next round you will bid spades.

However, partner opens one heart and you hold:

$$\spadesuit \text{K J 4 2} \quad \heartsuit \text{8 6} \quad \diamondsuit \text{K 9 6 4 2} \quad \clubsuit \text{J 7}$$

Bid one spade. You are not strong enough to respond at the two-level.

With two five-card suits bid the higher-ranking one first.

Partner opens one club. You hold:

$$\spadesuit \text{Q 9 6 4 3} \quad \heartsuit \text{A K 8 6 5} \quad \diamondsuit \text{9} \quad \clubsuit \text{Q 7}$$

Respond one spade. Partner could hold:

$$\spadesuit \text{K 8} \quad \heartsuit \text{Q 9 3} \quad \diamondsuit \text{A 8} \quad \clubsuit \text{K J 9 7 5 4}$$

PARTNER	YOU
1♣	1♠
2♣	2♥
2NT	3♥
4♥	Pass

After responding one spade you bid the hearts twice and reach your eight-card major-suit fit. Notice that four hearts is a good contract but three notrump will go down with a diamond lead.

50

With two or three four-card suits the general rule is to bid "up the line." In other words bid the cheaper four-card suit first.

Partner opens one club. You hold:

♠ A Q 6 5　♥ Q 8 6 4　♦ 6 5　♣ 8 5 2

Respond one heart. If partner has four hearts he will raise you immediately. If he cannot raise you he will bid one spade if he has four cards in that suit. In either case you will have found your four-four major suit fit if one exists. Notice that if you respond one spade with this hand you could easily miss a four-four heart fit.

Partner opens one club. You hold:

♠ K 9 6 2　♥ K 9 6 2　♦ Q 6 4 2　♣ 8

Bid one diamond. Partner will rebid one heart or one spade if he has a four-card major and you will then give him a single raise next round.

Partner opens one club. You hold:

♠ 8 5　♥ K J 9 5　♦ Q 9 6 2　♣ 8 6 5

Respond one heart. This hand is worth only one bid. Bid the major while you have the chance. If you respond one diamond, there is a possibility that your left hand opponent will bid one spade and you will never find the heart fit if it exists. This an exception to the up-the-line rule: A minimum hand with four diamonds and a four-card major bids the major

Quiz on Responding

Partner deals and bids one diamond. Next hand passes. What do you bid with the following?

1.　♠ Q J 6 4　♥ 8　♦ 9 8 7　♣ A J 9 8 2

2.　♠ 8 6 3　♥ J 8　♦ A K 8 7　♣ 9 8 6 2

3.　♠ Q J 2　♥ K 8 7　♦ A 9 7　♣ Q 7 6 2

51

4. ♠ 8 6   ♥ K Q 8 7   ♦ 7 6   ♣ A K J 6 5

5. ♠ A K 4 2   ♥ J 7 5 3   ♦ 7 5 2   ♣ 7 5

Partner deals and bids one spade. Next hand passes. What do you bid with the following?

6. ♠ 7   ♥ Q J 9 8 5   ♦ 8 3   ♣ K J 9 5 4

7. ♠ A Q 7 5   ♥ 9 8   ♦ K J 7 5   ♣ 9 6 2

8 ♠ Q 9 6 5 2   ♥ 2   ♦ 9 2   ♣ K Q 9 7 5

Answers to Quiz

1. Bid one spade. You do not have enough strength to bid at the two level.

2. Bid two diamonds, showing 6-9 and denying four of a major. This raise usually shows five diamonds, but the alternative of one notrump is unattractive with weakness in both majors.

3. Bid two notrump, showing a balanced 10-12 and denying a four-card major. Partner will only pass with a dead minimum.

4. Bid two clubs and plan to bid hearts next round. You will then have shown four hearts and longer clubs. (Your second suit is always assumed to be four unless you rebid it.)

5. Bid one heart. Go up the line with four-card suits. If you bid one spade here, a four-four heart fit might get lost.

6. Bid one notrump. Not ideal but the only choice. You show 6-9 and deny a fit with partner. This does not promise a balanced hand.

7. Bid three spades, a limit raise. This shows four trumps and a hand worth 10-12.

8. Bid four spades, a shut-out bid. This shows five-card support for partner's major and not much on the side.

7

Points Schmoints! and The Art of Rebidding

South deals and opens one spade holding:

♠ A 9 8 5 4 3 2   ♥ A Q 2   ♦ —   ♣ 9 8 7

The bidding proceeds as follows:

SOUTH	WEST	NORTH	EAST
1♠	Pass	2♠	3♥
3♠	Pass	Pass	Pass

West leads a heart and dummy comes down with:

♠ K 10 7 6   ♥ 7 6   ♦ J 7 5 2   ♣ Q 6 3

South is embarrassed to discover that even a half-wit could scarcely fail to make ten tricks here. North is righteously indignant about the matter, having strained to raise partner on a dead minimum. If South makes the plaintive excuse, "My hand was only worth thirteen points, partner," North is likely to sneer,

"Points Schmoints!"

This is Expertise. Translated into English it means "Only an idiot counts points! Why don't you learn to use your head?"

North is only partially correct. Experts do count points. But they are not slaves to the point count. They adjust their evaluation of the hand as the bidding progresses.

53

In the above example, South should see that once spades have been supported, he will probably win seven trump tricks in his own hand. And once East has bid hearts, the finesse in that suit figures to work. Even if North has a minimum raise there should be a good play for game.

The point count did not let South down, however. He simply forgot to adjust his points as the bidding proceeded. As we have seen earlier, assets double with a nine-card fit and triple with a ten-card fit. In this case South's three assets, (one for the long suit and two for the void), have tripled with the known ten-card fit, and A Q 2 has become the equivalent of A K 2. South's total worth is now twenty and North has promised at least six. A bid of four spades is justified.

Here is another example. You hold:

♠ 6   ♥ K J 8 6 5 4 2   ♦ 7 5   ♣ K Q 4

The auction has started:

PARTNER	YOU
1♦	1♥
1NT	?

What do you bid?

You picture partner with a balanced 12-14. He should have at least two hearts, therefore you have a nine-card fit and your two assets have doubled to four. Add in your nine high-card points and you get to thirteen, enough for game opposite an opening bid. Bid four hearts.

If you want to bid like an expert you must continually readjust your points. Do not forget to add a strong dash of common sense. And if you want to SOUND like an expert you will have to do it all mentally. Do not mention the assets. When you talk about points, refer only to high-card points.

Rebids by Opener

When you open the bidding with one of a suit and partner raises your suit to any level, or bids any number of notrump, you become captain because you know almost exactly what he has. Usually you can place the final contract right away.

Always keep in mind those three landmarks:

26 points make a game.
33 points make a small slam.
37 points make a grand slam.

Example 1. YOU   PARTNER
            1♠   2♠
            ?

You hold: ♠ A Q J 8 6   ♥ K Q 4 2   ♦ 9 7 6   ♣ 8

Pass. Partner's hand is worth 6-9. When you know the partnership total is less than 26, pass at the first convenient opportunity.

Example 2. YOU   PARTNER
            1♠   2♠
            ?

You hold: ♠ A Q J 6 4 2   ♥ A 8 5   ♦ 5   ♣ K Q 10

Bid four spades. Your two assets have doubled to four. When you add in the high-card points, your hand is worth 20 and partner has promised at least six.

Example 3. YOU   PARTNER
            1♠   3♠
            ?

You hold: ♠ A Q 9 7 5   ♥ 8   ♦ A K 10   ♣ A Q J 3

Bid six spades. Partner has made a limit raise showing four trumps and a hand worth about 11. With all suits controlled you do not need Blackwood. Your two assets have doubled to four, and you can count to more than 33.

Example 4. YOU   PARTNER
            1♦   1NT
            ?

You hold: ♠ A 9 2   ♥ 7   ♦ A Q 9 8 6 2   ♣ Q 9 3

Bid two diamonds. Game is unlikely as partner has only 6-9. If your hand were more balanced you would pass one notrump. But with a six-card suit it is usually better to play in two of your suit.

The above examples were all cases where partner had limited his hand and you were able to place the contract immediately. Sometimes you will need to ask him a question.

Example 5.

YOU	PARTNER
1♠	1NT
?	

You hold: ♠ A Q 9 7 6   ♥ K J 8   ♦ K 6   ♣ A J 8

Bid two notrump. Partner has shown 6-9. You are asking him to go to game with a maximum, (8-9), or pass with a minimum, (6-7).

Example 6.

YOU	PARTNER
1♠	2♠
?	

You hold: ♠ A J 9 7 6 2   ♥ A 6   ♦ Q 4   ♣ K Q 10

Bid three spades. This asks partner to go to game with a maximum and pass with a minimum.

So far we have been discussing cases where partner has limited his hand by raising you, or by bidding some number of notrump. What about the times when partner bids a new suit? Suppose the bidding starts:

YOU	PARTNER
1♦	1♥

In this case both your hand and partner's are virtually unlimited. You each have only the vaguest notion of what the other has. Your rebid may be the key to the whole auction.

Minimum Rebids

With a minimum opening bid you must be careful not to push the auction too high. Partner may have responded on six points in which case a contract of seven or eight tricks is high enough. A rebid of one notrump or a single raise of partner's suit or a rebid of two of your own suit all show that your opening bid was a minimum. A rebid in a new suit which is cheaper than two of your first suit MAY OR MAY NOT be a minimum.

Rebids That Always Show a Minimum

A		B		C	
YOU	PARTNER	YOU	PARTNER	YOU	PARTNER
1♦	1♥	1♦	1♥	1♦	1♥
1NT		2♥		2♦	

In sequence A your rebid of one notrump shows a minimum balanced hand, not strong enough to open one notrump. In other words, 12-14. You have also denied a four-card spade suit. Partner is now the captain and should be able to place the contract.

In sequence B you have shown a minimum hand. Again partner is captain as he knows much more about your hand than you do about his. You are likely to have four hearts, but occasionally you have only three. Always raise with four, sometimes with three.

In sequence C you have shown a minimum hand with a six-card diamond suit. (When you bid your first suit twice you normally show six). And you have also denied a four-card major. Partner is captain.

The next two sequences may or may not show a minimum.

D		E	
YOU	PARTNER	YOU	PARTNER
1♦	1♥	1♦	1♥
1♠		2♣	

In sequence D you might have a minimum such as:

♠ A Q 8 7   ♥ 7 4   ♦ A Q 8 6 2   ♣ 8 6

or you might have a strong hand such as:

♠ A K 8 6   ♥ 9   ♦ A K Q J 8   ♣ 7 5 2

Similarly in sequence E you could have a minimum hand or a strong one:

♠ 6 5   ♥ 5 3   ♦ A Q 9 6 5   ♣ A Q 7 4

or   ♠ A 9   ♥ —   ♦ A J 8 6 4 2   ♣ A K J 8 6

There is as yet no captain in auctions D and E. But note that the opener almost always has at least five diamonds.

Strong Rebids

F		G		H	
YOU	PARTNER	YOU	PARTNER	YOU	PARTNER
1♣	1♠	1♣	1♠	1♣	1♠
2NT		3♠		3♣	

In sequence F, two notrump shows a hand that was too strong to open one notrump, but not strong enough to open two notrump. In other words you have a balanced 18-19 with stoppers in both unbid suits. This is a very strong bid but not forcing. Partner is now captain.

In sequence G you are showing four-card spade support and a hand worth about 17:

♠ A Q 7 5   ♥ 8 4   ♦ K 5   ♣ A Q J 8 6

Your jump is not forcing. So if you had a slightly stronger hand you would rebid four spades, not three spades. Partner is now captain.

In sequence H you are showing a strong six-card club suit and a hand worth about 17. Again it is not forcing and partner is now captain.

Stronger Rebids

I		J	
YOU	PARTNER	YOU	PARTNER
1♦	1♠	1♦	1♠
3♣		2♥	

In sequence I, three clubs is a jump shift, (a jump into a new suit), which is forcing to game. You are saying that you have enough to make game even if partner has only six points.

In sequence J your two-heart bid is a reverse. (You have bid your suits in reverse order, the lower-ranking before the higher-ranking, in

58

such a way that partner will have to go to the three-level to take you back to your first suit.) Notice that if partner simply wants to give a preference to your first suit he has to bid THREE diamonds just as he does in sequence I. Partner assumes you have four hearts and longer diamonds.

The reverse is forcing for one round but it is not forcing to game. The reverser usually has at least 17 HCP.

Jumps to Game by Opener

K		L	
YOU	PARTNER	YOU	PARTNER
1♣	1♠	1♣	1♠
4♠		3NT	

Sequence K is much like sequence G except that your hand is worth about twenty points instead of seventeen. You believe that game can be made even if partner has only six points. You could hold:

♠ A Q 9 6   ♥ 8 7   ♦ A Q   ♣ A Q J 8 5

Partner is now captain and in charge of any further investigation.

Sequence L is a special case. Your bid of three notrump does NOT show a balanced hand with a specific range of points. These balanced ranges are already provided for. (See Chapter 3).

Instead, the three notrump bid in L shows a hand which will probably take nine tricks based on a long running club suit. You might hold:

♠ 7   ♥ A Q 6   ♦ K 9 8   ♣ A K Q 10 9 8

If partner contributes one trick you will probably make three notrump. Notice that if partner is considering slam he should opt for notrump or clubs, not spades.

59

Preference

Suppose you have:

♠ A 9 6 4 2   ♥ 9 8 5 3   ♦ 5 2   ♣ Q 6

PARTNER	YOU
1♦	1♠
2♣	?

You cannot bid two spades, which would guarantee six cards. You cannot bid two hearts or two notrump, both of which would show far stronger hands. You are tempted to pass, but that would also be wrong. Your partner may have just four clubs, and will be outnumbered in the trump suit. When that happens, something has gone wrong with your bidding.

The right bid is two diamonds, which is in no way positive and shows no extra strength. Your partner has virtually guaranteed at least five diamonds: When he refused to bid one notrump he showed an unbalanced hand.

Your bid is a preference, and is weak. The message is: "I am going back to your first suit because I know it may be longer than your second suit and cannot be shorter."

When partner offers you a choice of suits and you are weak, go back to his first suit as cheaply as possible UNLESS you are longer in the second suit. Preference at the same level often shows two cards.

Quiz on Rebids

What is your rebid with each of the following?

1. | YOU | PARTNER |
    |-----|---------|
    | 1♦ | 1NT |
    | ? | |

    You hold: ♠ A J 9 8   ♥ K Q 6   ♦ K 8 6 4   ♣ 7 6

2. | YOU | PARTNER |
    |-----|---------|
    | 1♦ | 2♣ |
    | ? | |

    You hold: ♠ K Q 5   ♥ K 8 7   ♦ A J 8 5 2   ♣ 8 7

3. YOU   PARTNER
   1♦   1♥
   ?

You hold: ♠ A Q 5   ♥ J 7   ♦ A Q J 8 7   ♣ K J 7

4. YOU   PARTNER
   1♠   2♥
   ?

You hold: ♠ A Q 10 8 7   ♥ K 8 7   ♦ A 6 2   ♣ 6 5

5. YOU   PARTNER
   1♦   1♥
   ?

You hold: ♠ A 4   ♥ 6   ♦ A K J 6 4   ♣ A J 5 4 2

6. YOU   PARTNER
   1♣   1♦
   ?

You hold: ♠ A Q 9 8   ♥ J 8 3 2   ♦ 7 6   ♣ A Q 7

7. YOU   PARTNER
   1♣   1♠
   ?

You hold: ♠ 8 6   ♥ A Q J 7   ♦ J 8 7   ♣ A J 7 6

8. YOU   PARTNER
   1♣   1♠
   ?

You hold: ♠ A Q J 10   ♥ J 6   ♦ 7 6   ♣ A J 6 4 2

9. YOU   PARTNER
   1♦   1♥
   ?

You hold: ♠ 8 7   ♥ A J 6 5   ♦ A Q J 8 5   ♣ A 9

10. YOU   PARTNER
   1♥   1♠
   ?

You hold: ♠ A J 8   ♥ A Q J 10 8   ♦ A K 7   ♣ 6 4

Answers to Quiz

1. Pass. Partner has 6-9 and no four-card major. One notrump is high enough.

2. Two notrump. Your minimum notrump rebid shows a balanced hand that was not strong enough to open one notrump. (In other words, 12-14).

3. Two notrump. Your jump to two notrump shows a balanced hand that was too strong to open one notrump. (In other words 18-19).

4. Three hearts. A two-heart response to one spade, always shows five (or more) hearts. Thus it is normal to raise with three.

5. Two clubs. This is a tremendous hand but it deteriorated when partner bid your singleton.

6. One heart. If you bid one spade or one notrump you might miss a heart fit.

7. One notrump. It is a shame not to mention that lovely heart suit, but you are not nearly strong enough to reverse into two hearts.

8. Two spades. Shows spade support and a minimum opening bid.

9. Three hearts. This is highly invitational but not forcing.

10. Three diamonds. This hand is worth twenty points and belongs in game now that you know partner has at least six. Four spades will be good if partner has a five-card suit. Four hearts will be good if partner has three. And three notrump will be good if partner has clubs controlled. It would be foolish to jump to four spades, four hearts or three notrump yourself because you might pick the wrong one. By making a jump shift you can force partner to make another bid which will probably clear up the whole problem. Occasionally, a jump shift has to be made on a three-card suit.

8

Opening Bids of More Than One of a Suit

Weak Two-Bids

Today it is standard to play an opening bid of two spades, two hearts or two diamonds as a weak two-bid. A typical hand might look like this:

Hand #1. ♠ 8 ♥ K Q 10 8 6 2 ♦ K 10 3 ♣ 7 5 2

You open two hearts and partner becomes the captain, because he knows a great deal about your hand and you know nothing about his. He assumes you have a good six-card suit and a hand that is not strong enough to open one heart. You figure to have about 6-10 high card points. And you should not have four cards in the other major. You may or may not have a nice looking honor on the side like that king of diamonds.

Partner can usually place the contract immediately, but occasionally he will have to ask you a question. (New suits and 2NT are both forcing.) For example, if he bids two spades he is saying "How do you like the idea of playing in spades?"

YOU	PARTNER
2♥	2♠
?	

With hand #1 you would turn the suggestion down by retreating to three hearts. Exchange your black-suit holdings however, and you would happily raise the spades.

Or suppose partner bids two notrump over your two hearts. This is forcing and artificial and asks whether you are maximum or minimum. With a maximum you bid a side feature.

YOU	PARTNER
2♥	2NT
?	

With hand #1 you bid three diamonds to show the diamond king. With the same hand without the diamond king you would make the discouraging rebid of three hearts, to show a minimum.

If by any chance you are lucky enough to hold:

♠ 8 7   ♥ A K Q 8 5 2   ♦ 5 4   ♣ 7 5 3

You would open this with two hearts and over partner's two notrump inquiry you would bid three notrump showing specifically AKQxxx.

Partner may choose to play for nine tricks at notrump opposite this.

Suppose partner raises your hearts:

YOU	PARTNER
2♥	3♥
Pass	

Here partner is NOT inviting you to bid game. He is simply trying to make life more difficult for the opponents. You must pass and leave all future decisions to him.

Quiz on Weak Two-Bids

On each of the following hands (nobody vulnerable), partner opens the bidding with two spades and your right-hand opponent passes. What do you bid?

1. ♠ 6   ♥ A Q 5 6   ♦ K J 7 2   ♣ Q J 5 3

2. ♠ A 7 4 2   ♥ 5   ♦ K Q J 8   ♣ K J 3 2

3. ♠ A 8 3 2   ♥ 5   ♦ K 7 5 2   ♣ J 7 5 2

4. ♠ A 8   ♥ Q J 4 3   ♦ A K Q 4   ♣ 7 5 2

Answers to Quiz on Weak Two-Bids

1. Pass. You have a minimum opening bid. Partner has less than an opening bid. There is no fit. You will be very lucky to make eight tricks.

2. Four spades. You hope to lose only a heart, a diamond and a club.

3. Four spades. This time you know that the opponents can make 11 or maybe 12 tricks in hearts. By bidding four spades immediately you make it much harder for them to get there. If partner has to play four spades doubled, he will probably make six spade tricks in his hand plus a couple of heart ruffs in dummy for -300 which is better than -450 and a lot better than -980.

   When you have support for your partner's weak two-bid you should almost always raise, whether you are weak or strong. If you go down, it is likely that the opponents would have made something.

4. Two notrump. You need to know whether partner has a minimum or a maximum, so you ask. If partner bids three spades, showing a minimum, you will pass. If he does anything else, showing a maximum, you will bid four spades.

Defense to the Weak Two-Bid

When an opponent opens with a weak two-bid the best defense is to treat it much like a one-bid. In the following examples your right-hand opponent deals and opens two hearts. What do you bid?

1. ♠ A K Q 9 4   ♥ 6 5 2   ♦ A J 8   ♣ 7 4

2. ♠ A J 9 6   ♥ 6 5   ♦ A 9 7 5   ♣ K Q 2

3. ♠ K 10 7   ♥ A Q 6   ♦ K J 6 4   ♣ A 10 7

4. ♠ 9 8   ♥ A Q 10 8 4   ♦ 7 6 4   ♣ K Q J

Answers

1. Bid two spades.

2. Double. Doubles of weak two-bids are always for take-out.

3. Bid two notrump. This shows that you would have bid one-no-trump had the opening bid been one heart.

4. Pass. If you double, partner will play you for something like hand 2. You must pass and hope that partner, who is short in hearts, will have enough to double. Then you will happily pass for penalties.

The Artificial Opening Bid of Two Clubs

Occasionally, you will pick up a hand that is so strong you expect to make game with practically no help from partner.

Example #1.

WEST	EAST	WEST	EAST
♠ A K J 10 6	♠ 8 4	2♣	2♦
♥ A K 10 9 8	♥ J 7	2♠	2NT
♦ 5	♦ K J 6 4	3♥	3♠
♣ A K	♣ Q 9 5 3 2	4♥	4♠
		Pass	

West opens two clubs which is strong and artificial. East almost always responds two diamonds (artificial), which is either negative or waiting. In order to respond something other than two diamonds, East needs 8 or more points and a good five-card or longer suit. (It is valuable to have the agreement that a "good" suit in this context is defined as one containing two of the top three honors.)

West now bids two spades, the higher-ranking of two suits of equal length. East shows scattered values but denies three-card spade support by bidding two notrump. West shows his second suit and East gives a preference to spades. West tries again with four hearts, but East shows no enthusiasm and they settle in four spades which is high enough.

Example #2.

WEST	EAST	WEST	EAST
♠ A K Q J 4 2	♠ 10 5 3	2♣	3♦
♥ 3	♥ A 3	3♠	4♠
♦ A J 3	♦ K Q 10 7 5	4NT	5♦
♣ A J 4	♣ 8 3 2	7NT	

Here is one of the rare situations where responder bids something other than the artificial two diamonds. Three diamonds shows a positive with a five-card or longer diamond suit, including two of the top three honors. It is this knowledge that allows West to count thirteen tricks, once he has located the heart ace.

Cheaper Minor = Second Negative

Suppose East has a very bad hand. Experienced players use what is called cheaper minor to show the real dog.

Example #3. Partner opens two clubs and you hold:

♠ J 9 7 2   ♥ 8 6 4   ♦ 5 4 2   ♣ 8 6 4

You respond two diamonds and if partner rebids two notrump (22-23), you pass gratefully. But if he rebids two hearts you cannot pass because it is forcing. Here is where you thank your stars for cheaper minor and bid three clubs.

PARTNER	YOU
2♣	2♦
2♥	3♣
3♦	3♥
4♥	Pass

Your three-club bid says "Partner, my hand is TERRIBLE! I have no aces and no kings and at most one queen." Once you get this off your chest you will feel much better about the auction. Partner shows his second suit, you have an easy preference to three hearts and partner bids the game. Maybe he will make it.

If partner's suit is spades the second negative is still three clubs. And if partner's suit is clubs the second negative is three diamonds. But if partner's suit is diamonds there is no general agreement about a second negative. For this reason experienced players think twice before opening two clubs when their suit is diamonds.

The best feature of the second negative is the inference available when you do not use it. Look again at example #1. The fact that East did not bid three clubs over two spades means that he must have some values.

Raising Partner's Suit

Partner opens two clubs and you respond two diamonds. Partner now bids two spades and you have support.

PARTNER	YOU
2♣	2♦
2♠	?

What do you bid with each of the following?

1. ♠ Q 9 6 4   ♥ 6 5   ♦ J 8 5 3   ♣ 7 6 5

2. ♠ 9 6 4 2   ♥ 6 5 3   ♦ 8 6 2   ♣ 4 3 2

3. ♠ Q 9 5   ♥ K 6   ♦ J 9 6 4   ♣ 8 6 5 2

4. ♠ Q 9 5   ♥ 7 6   ♦ A K 8 6   ♣ 8 6 4 2

Answers

1. Bid four spades. This shows good trump support but a very bad hand: no aces, no kings, no singletons and no voids.

2. Bid three clubs, the second negative. Whatever happens next you will take him back to spades.

3. Bid three spades, agreeing the trump suit. But make no aggressive moves thereafter. For example, if partner bids four clubs over your bid of three spades you will simply sign off with four spades. He will know you have some values because you did not use the second negative.

4. Bid three spades, agreeing the trump suit. This time however you will cue-bid the diamond ace next round. And if given a chance you will cue-bid the diamond king on the next round.

When partner opens two clubs it is generally a poor idea to respond in notrump. There are two reasons. In the first place, it is better to have the stronger hand concealed. (No matter how good your hand is, partner's is better.) In the second place, if the hand belongs in notrump the level can be determined more accurately by letting the strong hand initiate the notrump.

	A		B	
Example #4.	WEST	EAST	WEST	EAST
	2♣	2♦	2♣	2♦
	2NT	?	3NT	?

West's bidding on both sequences is very precise. (See chapter 3.) If East had bid two notrump instead of two diamonds he would be interfering with this narrow-range machinery. Once he has bid two diamonds he can easily add his points to partner's and place the final contract.

Preemptive Bidding

We have discussed weak two-bids which normally show a six-card suit. They are preemptive in nature because they deprive the opponents of bidding space. Three-level opening bids usually show a seven-card suit. They deprive the opponents of even more bidding space. Four-level opening bids tend to show an eight-card suit and they make life downright miserable for opponents.

Example #1. ♠ K Q J 9 8 6 5 4   ♥ 2   ♦ 9 8   ♣ 3 2

This is an ideal preempt because if spades are trumps you can expect to win seven tricks. And if spades are not trumps you may take no tricks. Clearly you should be willing to pay the opponents to let you play this hand in spades and the mechanics of scoring are such that the right price to offer is 500 points.

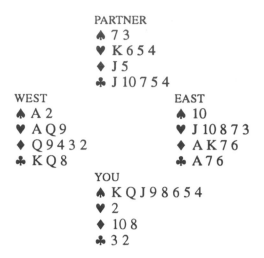

```
                    PARTNER
                    ♠ 7 3
                    ♥ K 6 5 4
                    ♦ J 5
                    ♣ J 10 7 5 4
        WEST                    EAST
        ♠ A 2                   ♠ 10
        ♥ A Q 9                 ♥ J 10 8 7 3
        ♦ Q 9 4 3 2             ♦ A K 7 6
        ♣ K Q 8                 ♣ A 7 6
                    YOU
                    ♠ K Q J 9 8 6 5 4
                    ♥ 2
                    ♦ 10 8
                    ♣ 3 2
```

East-West are vulnerable and you deal. As you expect to win seven tricks if spades are trumps you can afford to bid four spades. If you are allowed to play four spades doubled, you will lose 500 points. Obviously this is a tremendous bargain because East-West belong in six diamonds or six hearts, worth 1370 or 1430 respectively.

Naturally East-West suspect that they are being swindled but it is very hard for them to start looking for their fit at the five-level. The higher the preempt, the harder it is for them to get together.

You will often see an inexperienced player bid only three spades with this hand. He has a parsimonious horror of going down 500 and hopes to get away for 300 instead. The penny pincher soon regrets his niggardliness, however. Over three spades, East-West have a much better chance of finding their slam. They cannot have good enough spades to be tempted to settle for three spades doubled. The bait is just not sweet enough.

What do you do when partner opens with a preempt? Simply add your tricks to the those shown by partner and act accordingly. If he opens the bidding with three hearts, (not vulnerable), you know he is overboard by three tricks (500 points if doubled.) In other words he expects to win six tricks if hearts are trumps. If you hold:

♠ A 5 4   ♥ 6 2   ♦ A K 6 3 2   ♣ A 7 6

You can contribute four tricks so you raise him to game. Partner probably holds something like this:

♠ 8 7   ♥ K Q 10 8 7 5 4   ♦ 5   ♣ 9 3 2

In all cases the partner of the preempter is the captain and is in complete charge of the rest of the auction. His is the responsibility to determine what can be made and whether or not to sacrifice. The preempter has already told his story and must hold his peace unless forced to bid. (A new suit by partner below the game-level is forcing.)

WEST	NORTH	EAST	SOUTH
3♥	Pass	3♠	Pass
?			

West must do something. If he is unable to raise spades he will have to rebid his hearts.

Here is a fine example of preemptive bidding from an all expert game:

East-West vulnerable.
South deals.

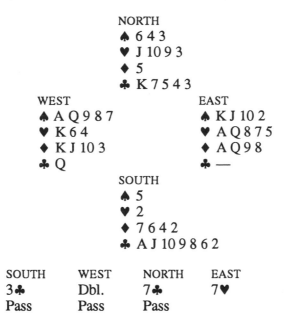

NORTH
♠ 6 4 3
♥ J 10 9 3
♦ 5
♣ K 7 5 4 3

WEST
♠ A Q 9 8 7
♥ K 6 4
♦ K J 10 3
♣ Q

EAST
♠ K J 10 2
♥ A Q 8 7 5
♦ A Q 9 8
♣ —

SOUTH
♠ 5
♥ 2
♦ 7 6 4 2
♣ A J 10 9 8 6 2

SOUTH	WEST	NORTH	EAST
3♣	Dbl.	7♣	7♥
Pass	Pass	Pass	

South started proceedings with a bid of three clubs and West doubled for take-out. North had no defense at all and he knew partner would be able to ruff a few diamonds in dummy so he upped the ante to seven clubs. Almost any non-vulnerable sacrifice is peanuts compared to the score for a vulnerable grand slam.

East now found himself on the horns of a dilemma. If North had frugally bid only six clubs, East would have had room to maneuver. He could then have bid seven clubs himself and forced West to choose a suit. West would have bid seven spades which would have made for a score of 2210. As it was East had a very tough decision to make. He guessed wrong when he bid seven hearts.

North naturally passed. He did not propose to give the enemy a chance to change its mind.

East-West could have made seven spades or seven diamonds. But in hearts North had to win a trump trick. So, thanks to excellent preemptive action, North-South came out with a plus score.

Moral: If your partner makes a preemptive opening and you have support, raise for all you are worth and a bit more.

Quiz on Preemptive Bidding

With each of the following hands you are the dealer and neither side is vulnerable. What do you bid?

1. ♠ 7   ♥ 8   ♦ K Q 9 8 7 5 4 3 2   ♣ 9 2

2. ♠ Q 4 3   ♥ J 8 6 5 4 3 2   ♦ J 7   ♣ 2

3. ♠ K Q J 10 5 4   ♥ 4   ♦ J 6   ♣ A 10 9 6

4   ♠ Q J 10 8 6 5 3   ♥ 8 7   ♦ —   ♣ J 10 9 7

5. ♠ J 10 8 7 5 4   ♥ K 9 7 6   ♦ A 5   ♣ 2

Answers to Quiz

1. Five diamonds. This is an ideal hand for a preempt. You expect to take eight tricks if diamonds are trumps and none if they are not.

2. Pass. I am all in favor of preemptive action, but this suit is just too anemic.

3. Bid one spade. Do not preempt when you have the values for a opening one-bid.

4. Bid three spades. You expect to win five spade tricks and one club.

5. Pass. You have too much defense on the side. Furthermore it is unwise to preempt with four cards in the other major. You may be preempting your own partner out of a good heart contract.

Defense to Opening Preempts

Doubles of opening preempts are for take-out up to and including four hearts. Doubles of four spades or higher suggest a penalty.

9

Competitive Bidding

About half the time you must expect an opponent to open the bidding. Of course, this does not mean that you automatically retire from the field of battle. It does mean, however, that the wrong action by you can be dangerous. If you do interfere and get caught it can be costly.

The most noticeable difference between the bidding of an expert pair and that of an average pair is the experts' agility in competitive situations. Experts are able to hop in and out of the auction on a high percentage of the hands and rarely get caught. Average players are much less aggressive in competitive situations and when they do butt in they frequently get punished. The reason is that experts have more defensive weapons at their command and know when and how to use them.

The Overcall

The most obvious defensive weapon is the simple overcall. Suppose your right-hand opponent, (R.H.O.), deals and opens the bidding with one diamond and you hold either of these hands:

1. ♠ 7 5   ♥ A K Q 9 8   ♦ 5 4   ♣ 10 8 6 2

2. ♠ A 5   ♥ K Q J 8 6   ♦ 9 7 6   ♦ A J 2

Bid one heart with both hands. The important consideration in deciding whether to overcall is not your point count but the quality of your suit. Nonvulnerable, at the one level a good five-card suit is all you need.

Overcalling at the Two-Level

R.H.O.	YOU
1♠	2♥

This time partner will assume you have a six-card suit and if you are vulnerable it should be a hefty one. Vulnerable you might hold:

♠ 7 5   ♥ A K J 10 7 5   ♦ A 7 5   ♣ 7 4

There are three good reasons to overcall.

1. Your side may be able to make more tricks than the opponents in which case your overcall becomes the first step in locating a suitable trump fit.

2. If partner has a bad hand with length in your suit, he may find a good sacrifice. Particularly at favorable vulnerability, (when the opponents are vulnerable and you are not), it may pay you to go down one or two or even three tricks, doubled, rather than allow the opponents to score a vulnerable game worth at least 600.

3. If L.H.O. gets to be declarer your overcall will help partner find the right opening lead. For this reason it is usually a losing proposition to overcall in a suit that you do not want led.

Jump Overcall

Suppose the bidding is:	R.H.O.	YOU
	1♣	2♠

What does your jump to two spades mean? Forty years ago you would have had a strong hand. Today strong jump overcalls have gone out with the horse and buggy: You are showing a weak hand with a decent six-card suit, much like an opening weak two-bid. Partner will act on the assumption that you have something like:

♠ K Q J 9 8 5   ♥ 8 7   ♦ 4 2   ♣ J 4 2

If you hold a seven-card suit:

♠ 8   ♥ K Q 10 9 6 5 3   ♦ 4 3   ♣ 9 8 7

The bidding will go:

	R.H.O.	YOU
	1♣	3♥

And partner will act on the assumption that you hold seven decent hearts and not much else.

Note that the definition of "decent" depends somewhat on the vulnerability. Not vulnerable most experienced players would jump to three hearts over an opponent's one club bid holding:

♠ 8   ♥ Q J 10 8 6 4 3   ♦ 6 5   ♣ 9 7 5

Suppose the bidding goes:

	R.H.O.	YOU
	1♣	4♠

Here you probably hold a hand that would have opened four spades as dealer. Vulnerable you might hold:

♠ K Q J 8 6 5 4 3   ♥ 8   ♦ J 10 9 6   ♣ —

If partner has nothing and you are doubled you expect to lose five tricks for a loss of 500.

In such situations, partner bids as if you had opened preemptively.

The One Notrump Overcall

R.H.O.	YOU
1♥	1NT

Here you are showing a hand that would probably have opened one notrump. The point count is a fraction stronger, 15-18 instead of 15-17, and you must have a stopper in R.H.O.'s suit.

Here is an ideal hand to bid one notrump over an opponent's one heart bid.

♠ K 8   ♥ A J 9   ♦ K Q J 8   ♣ Q J 10 7

Note: Over your notrump overcall partner can use Stayman or transfer just as if you had opened one notrump.

The Take-Out Double

Suppose the bidding is:

	R.H.O.	YOU
	1♦	Dbl.

It would be impractical to use this double for penalties, because the hand on which you could expect to punish a one-level bid in this situation hardly ever arises. Rather than keep the bid idle, players have been using the double of an opening suit-bid for take-out since the days of auction bridge.

Here your double of one diamond says, "I have an opening bid or better, partner. And I have at least three-card support for each of the other suits. Please tell me which of those suits is your longest?"

With ideal shape, meaning FOUR-CARD support for all three unbid suits, you can shade your point count to about eleven. A minimum take-out double of one diamond might look like:

♠ A J 7 5   ♥ A J 7 4   ♦ 8   ♣ J 9 5 2

There is no maximum. Great extra strength can compensate for imperfect shape. Double is the first move on most hands with 17 points or more, intending to bid again.

Responding to a Take-Out Double

You are South and the bidding has been:

WEST	NORTH	EAST	SOUTH
1♣	Dbl.	Pass	?

What do you bid with the following hands?

1. ♠ 9 5 4 2   ♥ 8 7   ♦ 9 7 4   ♣ 9 7 4 2

This is not a hand to be proud of, but partner has asked you to tell him which is your longest suit (not counting clubs) and you have no choice. The responsibility is his not yours. Bid one spade.

2. ♠ K 9 6 4   ♥ 8 6   ♦ K J 9 2   ♣ 8 7 6

With two suits of equal length, prefer the major. A minimum response here shows a hand worth about 0-8. Bid one spade.

3. ♠ A K Q 2   ♥ 8 6   ♦ J 5 4 2   ♣ 7 6 5

This is a different kettle of fish. Jump to two spades. This is invitational, not forcing. Partner will assume your hand is worth 9-11 and act accordingly.

4. ♠ Q 7   ♥ A Q 8 6 5 4   ♦ J 8 6 4   ♣ 7

You have at least a nine-card heart fit. This means your two assets, (one for the long suit and one for the singleton), have doubled, giving you a hand worth 13 points. Bid four hearts.

5. ♠ A 7   ♥ 8 7   ♦ 9 8 5   ♣ K Q J 9 8 7

Here is a rare situation where you disobey instructions and pass. This says "My clubs are better than West's clubs, partner. And if the final contract is one club doubled, please lead a club, so I can draw declarer's trumps before he scores any of his little clubs by ruffing something."

6. ♠ 9 6   ♥ K 8 7   ♦ J 7 5 2   ♣ K Q 10 4

This is the perfect opportunity to bid one notrump. Remember partner did not ask you to bid notrump. He asked you to bid your longest suit. So when you disobey him you need the opponent's suit well stopped and about 7-9 points. Replace your two kings with two spot cards and you would bid one diamond.

7. ♠ A 8 5 2   ♥ K J 7 2   ♦ K Q 7   ♣ 9 8

This is tricky. You know you belong in game, but which game? If you jump to four hearts it may turn out that partner has only three-card support and the same thing could happen if you jump to four spades. You obviously cannot jump to three notrump without a club stopper. The solution is to cue-bid the enemy's suit. Bid two clubs. This says nothing about clubs. It simply says "I think we have a game, partner, but I am not sure which game. You pick the suit."

After Partner Responds to Your Take-Out Double

When partner responds to your take-out double, always bear in mind that you forced him to bid. Suppose the auction has been:

WEST	NORTH	EAST	SOUTH
		1♦	Dbl.
Pass	1♥	Pass	?

As South you have made a take-out double of East's one diamond bid and partner has responded one heart. What do you bid with the following?

1. ♠ K Q 8 4   ♥ A 7 6   ♦ K 8   ♣ Q 8 5 2

2. ♠ K Q J 8   ♥ A 9 7 6   ♦ 5   ♣ K Q 5 2

3. ♠ K Q 10 8   ♥ A J 7 4   ♦ 8   ♣ K Q J 8

4. ♠ K Q J 9   ♥ A K 9 7 2   ♦ 8   ♣ A K Q

5. ♠ A Q 7 6   ♥ K Q 5   ♦ K 9 3   ♣ A Q 8

6. ♠ A Q 7 6   ♥ 7 2   ♦ K 9   ♣ A K J 9 2

Answers to Quiz

1. Pass. You bid your whole hand when you doubled. Partner has 0-8 so there is no game. If he has 0 he may be hard pressed to make one heart.

2. Bid two hearts. If partner has a maximum such as: ♠ 6 5 ♥ K 5 4 3 ♦ A 7 6 3 ♣ 8 7 2, there could be a game. And if he has nothing you should be safe at the two-level.

3. Bid three hearts. Partner will go on to game if he can contribute one trick.

4. Bid four hearts.

5. Bid one notrump. By doubling first and then bidding one notrump you show a hand that was too strong to simply overcall one notrump. You should have 19-21.

6. Bid two clubs. By doubling first and then bidding a new suit you show a strong hand (at least 17) and a five-card suit or longer. Remember, the double does not need perfect shape if the hand is very strong.

After an Opponent's Take-Out Double

When your right-hand opponent doubles your partner's opening bid, your action should be governed by one simple rule: With ten or more high-card points, redouble. With less than ten HCP make your natural call.

The bidding is:

NORTH	EAST	SOUTH	WEST
1 ♠	Dbl.	?	

What do you do as South with the following hands?

1. ♠ K Q 6 4   ♥ 7 2   ♦ K 8 6 2   ♣ 9 8 7

2. ♠ K Q 7   ♥ 9 6   ♦ 9 7 4 2   ♣ 9 8 4 2

3. ♠ A J 8   ♥ 8 7   ♦ A J 8 6   ♣ 9 7 6 5

4. ♠ 9   ♥ K Q 10 7   ♦ A 10 9 7   ♣ A J 9 7

5. ♠ 9 4   ♥ 9 4   ♦ K Q 10 9 8 4   ♣ Q 4 2

Answers to Quiz

1. Bid three spades. This shows four-card support but less than ten high-card points because you did not redouble.

2. Bid two spades. This shows slightly less than it would without the double.

3. Redouble and plan to bid two spades next round.

4. Redouble. Next round you plan to double the opponents in whatever they bid. Do not worry about playing one spade redoubled with a singleton. In the first place it is practically impossible for them to pass one spade redoubled. And even if they do partner will surely make at least seven tricks on power alone.

5. Bid two diamonds. This is not forcing as it denies ten high-card points.

The Double of One Notrump

The double of an opening notrump bid is primarily for penalties. The doubler should have 16 or more high-card points and in addition he should have a good lead in mind.

	EAST	SOUTH
	1NT	?

1. ♠ A K 8   ♥ 7 6   ♦ K Q J 10 8   ♣ A 8 2

2. ♠ A K 8   ♥ Q 7 6   ♦ K J 9 2   ♣ A 8 2

Hand 1. is a good double. You plan to lead the diamond king and even if partner is broke you expect to defeat one notrump. If partner actually has a few points, dummy will be broke and declarer will be carted off on a stretcher.

Hand 2. is a poor double even though you have 17 points. Every time you lead, you are probably helping declarer. And he will know from the double where all the cards are.

WEST	NORTH	EAST	SOUTH
1NT	Dbl.	Pass	?

When partner doubles one notrump you are expected to pass. An exception can be made when you have a long suit AND a terrible hand. Holding:

♠ 9 7   ♥ 9 6 2   ♦ 7 4 2   ♣ J 9 6 4 2

You probably do best to run to two clubs. Add a king and you would pass.

Negative Doubles

Thirty years ago it was standard to play penalty doubles of over-calls.

Example #1.

WEST	NORTH	EAST	SOUTH
1♦	1♠	Dbl	

In those days East held something like:

(A) ♠ K J 9 6 4 ♥ A K 8 ♦ 7 6 ♣ Q J 4

West was expected to pass and poor North-South were considerably out of pocket by the time the hand was over.

The trouble is that East seldom gets this golden opportunity. He is much more likely to hold something like this:

(B) ♠ 8 7 2 ♥ K J 8 6 ♦ 7 6 ♣ A 9 7 6

Playing penalty doubles of overcalls East would be stuck. He cannot bid one notrump without a spade stopper. He cannot bid two hearts without a five-card suit and at least ten points. The only thing he can do is pass and East-West may never find a possible heart or club fit.

Over the years penalty doubles of overcalls have gradually been abandoned in favor of a form of takeout double invented by Al Roth and called negative doubles. The negative double implies four cards in any unbid major. Today East will double with hand (B) to show that he would have bid one heart if North had passed.

At the one-level the negative double promises six or more high card points. At the two-level it should be slightly stronger, probably eight or more. And at the three-level you can expect ten or more.

You and partner must agree how high you want to play negative doubles. Let us assume you have agreed to play them through three spades. This means that any time you open one of a suit and the next player makes a natural overcall in a suit, up to and including three spades, a double by partner is takeout rather than penalty.

Let us look at some sequences:

Example #2.

WEST	NORTH	EAST	SOUTH
1♣	1♥	Dbl	

Here East is promising six or more points and exactly four spades. (With five spades he would bid one spade instead of doubling.)

Example #3.

WEST	NORTH	EAST	SOUTH
1♣	1♦	Dbl	

This time East should have four cards in each major. (If he had only one four-card major he would bid that one.)

Example #4.

WEST	NORTH	EAST	SOUTH
1♦	3♠	Dbl	Pass
?			

East has at least four hearts and ten or more points. If West has no heart fit and suitable spades, he may choose to leave the double in at this level.

Do not use a negative double when you have a natural bid available. Suppose East holds:

♠ 6 5   ♥ A Q J 8 7   ♦ A J 8   ♣ 7 5 4

The auction has been:

WEST	NORTH	EAST	SOUTH
1♣	1♠	?	

Bid two hearts. If you double here, partner will assume you either do not have the ten points required to bid at the two-level or you only have a four-card heart suit.

WARNING: Negative doubles do not apply when notrump is involved.

Example #5.

WEST	NORTH	EAST	SOUTH
1♥	1NT	Dbl	

East's double here is for penalties. He has ten or more points, South has a bunch of garbage, and North is in serious trouble.

Example #6.

WEST	NORTH	EAST	SOUTH
1NT	2♠	Dbl	

There are some pairs who agree to use this double as negative but it is still standard to play it for penalties.

NOW FOR THE GOOD NEWS: Go back to example #1 where East was happy to make a penalty double with hand (A). Playing negative doubles, East can probably have his cake and eat it too. All he has to do is pass. If West is short in spades he is expected to double for takeout. And East can convert this by passing. Here is another example:

Example #7.

WEST	NORTH	EAST	SOUTH
1♠	2♦	Pass	Pass
Dbl	Pass	Pass	Pass

WEST	EAST
♠ A K 9 8 5	♠ 7 2
♥ K 8 5 2	♥ Q J 4
♦ 6	♦ K J 9 7 5
♣ Q 7 5	♣ A K 9

When North overcalls two diamonds, East is thrilled. But he must not salivate all over the cards. This would be unethical because it would alert partner that he had something to salivate about. East must pass smoothly. Playing negative doubles opener is expected to reopen if he is short in the opponent's suit. Here West is short in diamonds so he reopens with a takeout double. North is not going to enjoy playing this.

Balancing

The art of reopening a dead auction is called balancing.

WEST	NORTH	EAST	SOUTH
1♦	Pass	Pass	?

In a good bridge game, South will seldom pass at this point. As East-West have died at one diamond, it is very likely that North-South have at least half the high-card points. Why should South sell out to one diamond when his side can probably score a partial in some other suit?

It requires substantially less strength to balance than to act in the immediate seat: The balancer knows that his partner must have some cards. Think of it as borrowing an ace from partner. In the above auction you are South and hold:

1. ♠ K 9 8 6   ♥ Q 7 5 2   ♦ 6 5   ♣ A 8 7

Once you have borrowed an ace from partner this becomes a perfect take-out double. By the way, when responding to your balancing double, partner must remember to discount four points from his hand and bid accordingly.

2. ♠ K 7 6   ♥ K 6 3   ♦ A Q 9   ♣ 9 7 5 2

Bid one notrump. In the balancing seat one notrump requires only about 11-14 points, with of course, a stopper in the enemy's suit.

3. ♠ A 8 4   ♥ K 8 2   ♦ A J 9   ♣ A J 8 6

You are too strong to bid one notrump in the balancing seat. You must double first and then bid notrump to show 15-18.

4. ♠ 7   ♥ A Q 9 7 5   ♦ K J 9 6 4   ♣ 9 7

Pass. You are delighted with diamonds as trumps. The odds are that East-West have a better contract. As a general rule when you have the opponent's suit it pays to maintain a discreet silence.

Other Balancing Situations

WEST	NORTH	EAST	SOUTH
1♥	Pass	2♥	Pass
Pass	?		

As North you hold:

♠ Q J 8 6   ♥ 8   ♦ A 7 5 3   ♣ J 10 7 6

You did not have enough to act over one heart. But now that East-West have died in a part score, it is clear that they do not have anything approaching 26 points. Partner figures to have at least 10 points. Rather than sell out to two hearts you should balance with a double. Perhaps South will bid two spades and go down one for -50. This is still better than -110 for two hearts making. Of course East-West may carry on to three hearts. This is fine. It is easier to defeat three hearts than two hearts.

For more modern defensive weapons see chapters 11 and 15.

10

Advanced Bidding

The Captaincy Principle

There are certain bids which give partner an almost exact picture of your hand. These include notrump bids, preemptive bids, raises of partner's suit, and, to a lesser extent, rebids of your own suit. Most new-suit bids are relatively imprecise because their range of meaning is so wide. Obviously, when you have a choice between the two it is better to choose the "exact" bid. For example, you hold:

♠ A Q   ♥ K J 8   ♦ A Q 9 8 7   ♣ 9 8 2

It would not be "wrong" to open one diamond but it would be inferior. The precise opening bid of one notrump is vastly superior.

As soon as one member of a partnership makes an "exact" bid, his partner is in the best position to place the final contract and therefore automatically becomes captain for the rest of the auction.

Hand #1.

WEST	EAST	WEST	EAST
♠ J 8	♠ K Q 10 9 5 2	1♣	1♠
♥ A J 9 3	♥ 7 2	1NT	4♠
♦ K J 7	♦ Q 10 5		
♣ K 9 8 7	♣ A 2		

West's one club bid is very imprecise. He could hold almost any number of clubs from three up and almost any number of high-card points from about ten up. East's one spade response is even more unlimited. He could hold almost any number of spades from four up and almost any number of high-card points from about four up.

86

West's no notrump rebid however is "exact". It shows a balanced hand with 12-14 points. East is now captain. He knows the partnership has enough for game but not slam. And he knows that there is at least an eight-card spade fit. No further investigation is necessary and he bids four spades.

It is not always possible to make an exact bid early in the auction. In a sequence such as:

WEST	EAST
1♠	2♦
2♥	3♣

All the bids are virtually unlimited and there is as yet no captain. The further the bidding advances without a captain, the more hazardous is the outcome. It is as though two people set out to sea in a small boat each determined to steer in his own direction. The sooner they elect a captain the more successful their journey will be.

Sometimes the captain will be able to place the contract immediately as in hand #1. Sometimes he will need to conduct a short investigation. Try this one:

Hand #2.

WEST	EAST	WEST	EAST
♠ A K J 9 5	♠ Q 6 4 2	1♠	2♠
♥ A K 2	♥ 9 7	3♦	3♠
♦ J 7 5 3	♦ 8 6 2	Pass	
♣ 9	♣ K Q 8 2		

West opens one spade and East raises him to two spades. This is an "exact" bid promising at least three trumps and a hand worth 6-9. West is now captain and he sees a good chance of game depending on where partner's points are.

He could bid three spades which would be a general-direction shot saying, "Bid game, partner, if you have a maximum." Instead he bids three diamonds. This says, "I am interested in game, partner, but I need help in diamonds." (Remember that new suits are forcing when you have already agreed upon a trump suit.)

Sadly, East has no help at all in diamonds. (Three small cards is the worst.) So he rejects the game try by bidding three spades which becomes the final contract. Declarer will probably lose three diamonds and a club.

Now suppose East's hand were instead:

♠ Q 6 4 2   ♥ 9 6   ♦ K Q 6   ♣ 9 7 5 2

He still has only seven points. But this time he knows the king and queen of diamonds are worth their weight in gold so he jumps to four spades and declarer will probably make an overtrick.

In slam bidding the same general principles apply. However as slams usually depend on aces and kings the emphasis here is on showing controls.

Hand #3.

WEST	EAST	WEST	EAST
♠ A K 8 6 4 2	♠ Q 9 7 3	1♠	3♠
♥ —	♥ J 9 3 2	4♣	4♦
♦ 10 8	♦ A K 5	6♠	Pass
♣ A Q 8 6 4	♣ J 10		

West opens one spade and East jumps to three spades showing four card support and 10-12 points. West is now captain. He knows he is in the slam zone but he is worried about losing two quick diamond tricks.

It would do little good to use Blackwood because if partner shows one ace, West will not know which ace it is. The solution is to bid four clubs. This says "I have the ace of clubs, partner and I am thinking of slam." East dutifully bids four diamonds to say he has the diamond ace and West bids the slam.

Here is another example.

Hand #4.

WEST	EAST	WEST	EAST
♠ K Q 8 7 4 2	♠ A 10 6 5	1♠	3♠
♥ A 3	♥ K 6 4	4♦	5♦
♦ A Q 8 6	♦ K 5	6♠	Pass
♣ 3	♣ J 8 6 2		

Again West opens one spade and East gives him a limit raise to three spades. West now bids four diamonds showing the diamond ace and interest in slam. East has a very attractive hand considering that he is known to have only about eleven. In slam bidding, aces and kings are much more important than lesser honors and East is blessed with an abundance of these important cards. But he does not dare bid four hearts for fear that partner will read him for the ace. And he does not want to bid four spades. In slam bidding a simple return to the trump suit is always discouraging. So he cue-bids five diamonds. As West has shown the ace of diamonds this is clearly the king.

West is delighted to hear about the diamond king and jumps to six spades. Notice that he is not worried about the spade ace. East could not make such an aggressive bid as five diamonds on an aceless hand with no high honor in trumps.

Hand #5.

WEST	EAST	WEST	EAST
♠ A 10 7	♠ K Q 9 8 5 2	1NT	2♥ (transfer)
♥ A 8 6 4	♥ 9	2♠	3♦
♦ K 8	♦ A J 9 7 2	4♠	4NT
♣ A 5 2	♣ 8	5♠	6♠

East becomes captain the minute that West opens one notrump. East starts with a transfer bid of two hearts and West obediently bids two spades. East now makes a try with three diamonds. West does not know yet whether it is a game try or a slam try but his job is to describe his own hand. With only a doubleton spade he would bid three notrump. With three spades but poor cards he would correct to three spades. With his actual hand, (three good spades, a plethora of aces, and the golden king of diamonds), he jumps to four spades. This persuades East to check for aces and bid the slam.

The Modern Style of Competitive Bidding

When the opponents have the stronger hands, winning strategy is to deprive them of bidding space. For this reason many jump bids which used to be strong are today played as preemptive. One example is the weak jump overcall discussed in the previous chapter.

Here is another situation.

WEST	NORTH	EAST	SOUTH
1♥	Pass	3♦	

This used to be a strong jump shift and it still is a strong jump shift. Note that there has been no competitive bidding here. East is thinking about a slam. However:

WEST	NORTH	EAST	SOUTH
1♣	1♥	3♦	

Today most experienced players use preemptive jump shifts in competition. If East had a good hand he could bid two diamonds which would be forcing and would save much-needed space for exploration. His actual bid of three diamonds resembles an opening bid of three diamonds. West is at liberty to pass.

WEST	NORTH	EAST	SOUTH
1♣	1♠	2♥	3♠

Here again experienced players use South's jump to three spades as preemptive. He promises four trumps and practically no defense. North is now captain and will decide how much to bid. A typical hand for South is:

♠ Q J 6 4   ♥ 7   ♦ Q 8 6 4 2   ♣ 9 7 2

Here are some hands where you have support for partner's overcall. The bidding has been:

WEST	NORTH	EAST	SOUTH
1♦	1♠	Pass	?

Nobody is vulnerable. What should South bid with:

1.   ♠ K 9 8   ♥ A 7 4 2   ♦ Q 9   ♣ 10 9 3 2

Bid two spades, just as you would have done if partner had opened the bidding with one spade.

2.   ♠ K 9 8   ♥ A 9 8 6   ♦ 9 8   ♣ A 6 4 2

This is too strong to bid two spades. You must cue-bid first. Bid two diamonds, the opponent's suit. This has nothing to do with diamonds. It just says you have a hand which is too strong for a single raise to two spades.

3.   ♠ A J 8 7 5   ♥ 8   ♦ 6 2   ♣ Q 8 7 6 2

Bid four spades, just as you would have done had partner opened the

90

bidding with one spade. It looks as if the opponents have missed their heart fit.

4. ♠ K Q 8 6   ♥ A Q 10 8 7   ♦ 9 7   ♣ K Q

You plan to bid game on this hand but you must cue-bid first. Bid two diamonds. Then jump to four spades next round. If you bid four spades immediately partner will think you have something like hand #3 where you are trying to shut out the opponents.

5. ♠ K J 8 5   ♥ 7   ♦ J 7 4 2   ♣ 10 8 6 2

Bid three spades, a weak jump response to the overcall.

6. ♠ A 8 6   ♥ 10 8 7 2   ♦ 9 7 6   ♣ 5 3 2

Pass! There is a limit to everything.

Making the Opponent's Overcall Work for You

Nobody is vulnerable and you are East.

WEST	NORTH	EAST	SOUTH
1♥	1♠	?	

Here is another competitive situation where experienced players use preemptive jump raises. What do you bid with the following hands?

1. ♠ 8 6   ♥ A J 8   ♦ A 8 6 2   ♣ 8 7 5 2

Bid two hearts, just as you would have done if North had passed.

2. ♠ 7   ♥ Q 8 7 6   ♦ J 9 7 5 2   ♣ 10 9 2

Bid three hearts. This is a typical weak jump raise. Partner can expect four trumps, usually a singleton somewhere, and not much else.

3. ♠ 8 6   ♥ K J 8   ♦ A K 8 6   ♣ 10 8 4 2

You are too strong to bid two hearts. You must cue-bid the opponent's suit. Bid two spades. This says nothing about spades. It merely shows heart support and a hand that is too strong for a single raise. (In other words, ten or more.) If partner does not wish to bid game opposite ten he will bid three hearts and you will pass.

4. ♠ 9 8   ♥ Q J 8 7 5   ♦ K 9 7 6 3   ♣ 8

Bid four hearts just as you would have done if North had passed.

5. ♠ 6 5 3 2   ♥ A J 8 6   ♦ A K J   ♣ Q 7

This time you belong in game or maybe even slam. But you cannot jump to four hearts right away or partner will think you have hand #4. First cue-bid two spades. If partner tries to sign off in three hearts you will of course carry on to game.

Try this auction:

WEST	NORTH	EAST	SOUTH
1 ♠	3 ♥	?	

Nobody is vulnerable. You are East and hold:

1. ♠ K Q 8 7   ♥ 7   ♦ A K J 8   ♣ 8 7 5 3

Cue-bid four hearts. You are too strong to bid either three spades or four spades.

Exceptions to the Weak Jump Overcall

Jump overcalls are not weak in the pass-out seat. Suppose the bidding has been:

WEST	NORTH	EAST	SOUTH
1 ♣	Pass	Pass	2 ♠

What does South's bid of two spades mean?

If North had bid two spades directly over West's one club bid, it would mean, "I have a weak hand, partner, with six decent spades, and I am trying to make it difficult for East-West to find their best game or even slam." But there is not much point trying to prevent East-West

92

from finding their best game or slam here. If South just says pass, East-West will never find ANY game or slam because the auction will be over. Common sense tells us that South's two-spade bid is not weak here. It is intermediate, showing a good opening bid with a good six-card suit. He might hold:

♠ A K J 9 7 5   ♥ 9 6   ♦ A K 8   ♣ 8 7

Here is another situation where the jump overcall is not weak.

WEST	NORTH	EAST	SOUTH
2♥	3♠		

West has announced to the world that he is weak and the hand probably belongs to North-South. It does not make sense for North to insist that he is weak and the hand probably belongs to East-West. Confucius say, "When both sides claim defeat, one side clazy."

After a weak opening bid a jump overcall is strong, not weak. It is highly invitational but not forcing. North might hold:

♠ A K Q 10 8 7   ♥ 8 7   ♦ A K J   ♣ 9 6

The S.O.S. Redouble

Even experts sometimes land in the soup. As a general rule, when this happens, the best policy is to lie still and take your licking. Any attempt to climb out usually makes matters worse.

WEST	NORTH	EAST	SOUTH
1NT	2♠	Dbl.	?

What do you bid as South, holding:

♠ 9   ♥ J 9 8   ♦ A 9 7 5 3 2   ♣ 9 6 2

Pass. To bid three diamonds is probably jumping from the frying pan into the fire.

Occasionally, when you are in trouble, you will be in the position of knowing that a sanctuary exists but not knowing where.

SOUTH	WEST	NORTH	EAST
1♣	Dbl.	Pass	Pass
?			

As South you hold:

♠ A 10 8 7   ♥ K Q 10   ♦ K J 9   ♣ 10 8 2

West has doubled one club for take-out and East has left it in, announcing to the world that his clubs are longer and stronger than yours. If you were happy to play one club doubled you would pass and the auction would be over.

It is logical therefore that a redouble by you in the pass-out seat says, "Help Partner! Please get me out of this by bidding your longest suit." It is called the S.O.S. redouble. North will bid something and whatever it is, will surely be better than one club doubled.

Warning: Do not confuse the immediate redouble with the S.O.S. redouble.

SOUTH	WEST	NORTH	EAST
1♣	Pass	Pass	Dbl.
Redbl.			

In this case South is not in the pass-out seat and he is not in trouble. He is showing a very strong hand.

94

11

The Gadgets

Standard American is basically a natural system of bidding. However experienced partnerships tack on a few artificial conventions or "gadgets." For example almost everyone plays Blackwood. Here bids of four and five notrump as well as all the responses are artificial bids.

Good pairs adopt a range of artificial devices. They choose the ones they feel are most useful, are easy to remember, and do not interfere with the rest of their bidding.

If you are a new duplicate player just starting out in the tournament world, you may be awed by the gadgets cropping up on all sides. Perhaps you will decide that if you are going to get anywhere in this jungle you had better grab as many gadgets for yourself as you can. You may even jump to the erroneous conclusion that if one gadget is good, fifty gadgets must be fifty times as good.

Forget it! The way to improve your bridge is to cut down on your mistakes. Fifty gadgets will get you nothing but one long headache.

So before you leap merrily into the gadget camp, remember that for each one you adopt there are two penalties to pay. First, you give up the natural meaning of the bid involved. Second, you put an additional tax on your memory and that of partner. Human memory is not infallible. When you are carrying too many conventions in your head you are apt to forget one in the heat of battle. And the catastrophe that can occur when a convention is forgotten can easily outweigh all the benefits ever derived from using it correctly. In the case of Blackwood, the penalties are very slight in comparison with the potential gain.

For example:

WEST	EAST
1♠	3♠
4NT	

Here the four notrump bid does not have much use as a natural bid.

95

Furthermore, it is such a "shocking" bid that it serves to jar the memory. Players are very unlikely to forget Blackwood.

In contrast, take a look at the popular Texas convention. Texas is a form of transfer bid over partner's opening notrump, much like the Jacoby transfer bid, but at the four-level instead of the two-level. Over an opening notrump, a jump to four diamonds requires opener to bid four hearts and a jump to four hearts requires him to bid four spades.

(A)	WEST	EAST	(B)	WEST	EAST
	1NT	4♦		1NT	4♥
	?			?	

Sequence (A) is no problem. West is quickly awakened by that unusual jump to four diamonds. But the four-heart bid in sequence (B) sounds so natural that a lethargic West could easily pass. And if he does pass the ensuing disaster may quickly persuade East-West to give Texas back to the Indians.

Blackwood

A bid of four notrump, (except when it is a direct raise of notrump), is conventional and asks partner to show how many aces he holds. The responses are as follows:

> With no aces or all four aces, bid five clubs.

> With one ace, bid five diamonds.

> With two aces, bid five hearts.

> With three aces, bid five spades.

At this point, if, and only if, all the aces are accounted for, the Blackwood bidder may now bid five notrump to ask for kings if he is interested in a grand slam. The responses are similar:

> With no kings or all four kings, bid six clubs.

> With one king, bid six diamonds.

> With two kings, bid six hearts.

> With three kings, bid six spades.

I am sometimes asked how is partner to tell whether you have no aces or all four aces when you bid five clubs? This reminds me of the story about the two biology majors:

First student: "What is the difference between an elephant and a butterfly?"

Second student: "I don't know."

First student: "So maybe you should major in something else?"

If partner cannot tell from the previous bidding whether you have no aces or all four aces he should give up bridge and try something else.

Most inexperienced players overwork the Blackwood convention. In general Blackwood should NOT be used as a means of getting to a slam. Before you use Blackwood you should already know that the partnership has sufficient values for slam. Blackwood should be used as a means of STAYING OUT OF A SLAM when two aces are missing.

Do not use Blackwood unless you know what you are going to do after partner responds. A player with a void, for example, should rarely use Blackwood because he may not know which ace partner is showing. And with the possibility of two quick losers in an unbid suit it is dangerous to use Blackwood.

Keep this in mind also. When the Blackwood bidder continues with five notrump he is not just asking about kings for his own amusement. The five notrump bid guarantees all the aces and indicates interest in a grand slam. Suppose East holds:

♠ K Q 8   ♥ 8 7 5   ♦ 7   ♣ A K Q 9 3 2

WEST	EAST
1 ♠	2 ♣
2 ♦	3 ♠
4NT	5 ♦
5NT	7 ♠

Once East knows that all the aces are accounted for he is able to bid seven himself.

If responder has a void he may show it if he thinks it will prove useful to partner. (A void in an opponent's suit is probably useful. A void in partner's suit is better ignored.)

One way to show a void is to give the correct Blackwood response, but at the six level instead of the five level. Thus over partner's

97

Blackwood, with two aces and a useful void, bid six hearts instead of five hearts. Some players, however, prefer to bid five notrump to show two aces and a void. With one ace and a void they jump to six of the void suit. If you have no agreement it may be better to ignore the void.

Never count a void as an ace. This is a sure recipe for disaster.

There are problems with Blackwood when clubs is the intended trump suit. Be careful.

Gerber

Gerber, like Blackwood, is a convention designed to find out how many aces partner has. Unlike Blackwood, Gerber is used in notrump auctions.

Suppose partner opens the bidding with one notrump and you hold:

♠ 6 ♥ K Q 8 7 5 4 3 2 ♦ K Q 10 ♣ J

Your only concern is the number of aces in partner's hand. If he holds four aces you plan to bid a grand slam. If he holds three aces you will bid six hearts. And if he has less than three aces you will stop at the four or five level.

You cannot use Blackwood, however, because four notrump directly over partner's one notrump is a quantitative raise of notrump. The solution is to use the Gerber four-club convention.

Over partner's opening notrump a jump to four clubs asks for aces. He replies as follows:

With no aces (or all four) he bids, four diamonds.

With one ace, he bids four hearts.

With two aces, he bids four spades.

With three aces, he bids four notrump.

If the Gerber bidder wishes to know about kings he continues by bidding five clubs and the replies are similar.

DO NOT MEMORIZE these replies. Just remember that with no aces you make the cheapest bid. With one ace you make the next cheapest bid. etc.

Suppose on the example hand the bidding proceeds:

PARTNER	YOU
1NT	4♣
4♦	?

Four clubs is Gerber and four diamonds shows zero or four aces. But partner cannot have zero aces because there are not enough points left for him to open one notrump without at least one ace. Count them. So partner has all four aces and you can count thirteen tricks. You might as well bid seven notrump.

Roman Keycard Blackwood

Today most experienced players use a form of Blackwood known as Roman Keycard, (RKC). The chief difference between regular Blackwood and RKC is that with the latter the king of trumps counts as an ace. There are thus five aces or key cards in the deck and the responses are:

Five clubs shows zero or three key cards.

Five diamonds shows one or four.

Five hearts shows two without the trump queen.

Five spades shows two with the trump queen.

Example:

WEST	EAST
♠ K Q 8 7	♠ A 9 6 4 2
♥ Q J	♥ A 4
♦ Q J 10 9 8 5	♦ A
♣ A	♣ K Q J 10 6

WEST	EAST
1♦	1♠
3♠	4NT
5♠	7♠

West opens one diamond and East bids only one spade. (It is not a good idea to make a jump shift with a two-suiter because it wastes space.) West jumps to three spades showing a hand worth about 17 with four trumps, and the only question in East's mind now is whether to bid six or seven. Fortunately the partnership has agreed to play RKC, and in response to four notrump West bids five spades showing two key cards and the queen of trumps. East happily bids the grand.

Notice that East would have a much harder row to hoe playing regular Blackwood.

The Grand Slam Force

Occasionally you will get a hand where a small slam seems assured and the only thing keeping you from bidding a grand slam is a possible trump loser. Suppose partner opens one spade and you hold:

♠ A 6 4 2   ♥ —   ♦ A K Q J 8 6   ♣ A 6 2

If partner has nothing but ♠ K Q 4 3 2, you expect to take thirteen tricks: five spades, six diamonds, one club and one heart ruff. A jump to five notrump in this situation is the GRAND SLAM FORCE. It says forget everything else, partner. Just look for the top three trump honors. If you have any two of these, please bid a grand slam in our suit. Otherwise, bid only six.

PARTNER	YOU
1 ♠	5NT
7 ♠	

This is your lucky day.
(See also page 160.)

The Unusual Notrump

Sometimes it is impossible for a notrump bid to have its normal meaning.

Example #1.

	WEST	NORTH	EAST	SOUTH
	1NT	2NT	Pass	?

Here North has obviously made an unusual bid. If he had a strong hand he would have doubled. If he had a one-suiter he would have bid his suit. The answer is that he has a two-suited hand and wants partner to choose between the two suits. In the United States the unusual notrump has long been associated with the two minor suits. In example #1 North should hold something like:

♠ 6   ♥ 7   ♦ K Q 10 9 5 4   ♣ A Q J 10 6

South is being asked to bid his longer minor.

Example #2.   WEST   NORTH   or   WEST   NORTH
　　　　　　　1 ♠   2NT   　　1 ♥   2NT

Here again North has made an unusual bid. It would be exceedingly rare for him to hold a standard two notrump opening when an opponent has opened the bidding. And if he did have such a hand he could always double first. The immediate jump to two notrump over an opponent's opening bid of a major shows both minors.
　　A jump bid of two notrump over an opening bid of a minor shows the two cheaper-ranking unbid suits.

Example #3.   WEST   NORTH
　　　　　　　1 ♦   2NT

North has clubs and hearts.

Example #4.   WEST   NORTH
　　　　　　　1 ♣   2NT

North has diamonds and hearts.

Example #5.   WEST   NORTH   EAST   SOUTH
　　　　　　　1 ♠   Pass   2 ♦   2NT

When two suits have been bid by the opponents, a bid of two notrump, (whether or not it is a jump), shows great length in the two unbid suits. In example #5, South holds clubs and hearts, at least 5-5. East-West appear to be on the way to game. Perhaps North-South can find a profitable sacrifice.

Example #6.   WEST   NORTH   EAST   SOUTH
　　　　　　　1 ♠   Pass   2 ♠   Pass
　　　　　　　Pass   2NT

101

When the bidding has died below game the unusual notrump may be used with slightly less distribution. Suppose North holds:

♠ 6 5 2　♥ 8　♦ A K 8 6　♣ Q J 8 4 2

He can not act directly over the opening bid. But when the opponents stop in two spades he would like to push them up a little higher. He cannot double for take-out because partner would surely bid hearts. So he bids two notrump asking partner to bid his longer minor.

Warning: The following auctions are NOT UNUSUAL.

Example #7.

WEST	NORTH
1 ♠	1NT

North's bid of one notrump shows a balanced 15-18 with spades stopped. There is nothing unusual about it.

Example #8.

WEST	NORTH
2 ♠	2NT

Again North has a hand that would have bid one notrump over the opponents one spade.

Exception:

WEST	NORTH	EAST	SOUTH
Pass	Pass	Pass	1 ♠
1NT			

Here one notrump is unusual. West can not possibly hold the requirements for a natural one notrump overcall because he is a passed hand. He must have both minors.

Michaels Cue-Bid

Thirty years ago the immediate cue-bid showed a powerhouse in the other suits. This was rarely useful and when the powerhouse did appear one could always substitute a takeout double. Today the immediate cue-bid is almost universally played to show a two-suiter. After a minor suit, the cue-bid shows at least 5-5 in the majors.

WEST	NORTH	or	WEST	NORTH
1 ♣	2 ♣		1 ♦	2 ♦

North holds something like:

♠ K Q J 8 6   ♥ A J 10 8 5   ♦ 8   ♣ 7 4

South will bid his longer major at whatever level his hand warrants.

Over a major suit, the cue-bid shows the other major and an unspecified minor.

WEST	NORTH	EAST	SOUTH
1♠	2♠	Pass	2NT
Pass	3♦	Pass	Pass
Pass			

North's bid of two spades shows hearts and a minor, at least 5-5. If South wants to know which minor he bids two notrump and North tells him.

Landy

When your right-hand opponent opens the bidding with one notrump it is dangerous to enter the bidding. There are many conventions invented for competing over an opponent's notrump and the simplest of these is Landy. Playing Landy, an overcall of two clubs over one notrump is an artificial bid showing both majors.

Example .

	WEST	NORTH	EAST	SOUTH
	1NT	2♣		

North holds something like:

♠ A Q 6 4 2   ♥ K J 8 6 5   ♦ K 7   ♣ 8

Without Landy it would be dangerous to compete here. It would be lunacy to overcall two hearts or two spades. If you pick the wrong suit you could be carried out on a stretcher. Playing Landy you bid two clubs and partner responds in his longer major. This all but eliminates the danger of playing in the wrong suit.

WARNING: When you play Landy you have to give up the natural overcall of two clubs to show clubs. This is not much of a sacrifice because if all you can make is two clubs, the opponents can easily outbid you. When you play Landy you give up the unimportant club suit in exchange for the two majors.

One Notrump Response to a Major Forcing

Today the majority of experienced players use one notrump as a one-round force over a major.

WEST	EAST
1♠	1NT
?	

East probably has 6-9 points, but occasionally he will have 10-12 in which case he will make an aggressive move at his second turn.

With each of the following you open one spade and partner responds one notrump (forcing). What is your rebid?

Hand #1. ♠ A Q 7 6 4   ♥ A J 7 5   ♦ 6 4 3   ♣ 7

Hand #2. ♠ A Q 7 6 4 2   ♥ K 7 6   ♦ K 8   ♣ 7 4

Hand #3. ♠ K Q 8 6 5   ♥ K 8 7   ♦ 8 7   ♣ A 6 2

With hand #1 rebid two hearts showing at least four hearts. With hand #2 rebid two spades showing a six-card suit. With hand #3 rebid two clubs. (You will frequently have to rebid a three-card minor.)

Now look at hands responder might hold.

Hand #1 ♠ 8 5   ♥ Q 7 5 2   ♦ K Q 9 8   ♣ J 6 2

Hand #2 ♠ 8   ♥ K J 9 8 6 5   ♦ J 7 6   ♣ J 7 5

Hand #3 ♠ A J 7   ♥ A 8 6   ♦ Q 10 9 2   ♣ 7 5 2

Hand #4 ♠ J 9   ♥ A Q 8   ♦ K 10 9 8   ♣ J 10 7 5

Hand #1 is an ordinary 6-9 notrump response to partner's opening bid of one spade. If partner rebids two spades or two hearts or two diamonds you will pass. If he rebids two clubs you will correct to two spades. (Remember that he could have only three clubs.)

104

With hand #2 partner will probably rebid two diamonds or two clubs and you will bid two hearts, showing a strong desire to play right there.

With hand #3 you bid one notrump, then jump to three spades next time. This shows three-card support and a hand worth 10-12.

With hand #4 you bid one notrump and plan to bid two notrump next time. This will show stoppers in the unbid suits and about 11 points.

Note: One notrump is not forcing by a passed hand.

Jacoby Two Notrump Response to a Major

When limit raises came into fashion, several substitutes were developed for the old-fashioned forcing raise (13-15). By far the most popular, and also the most effective method is that invented by Oswald Jacoby and known as JACOBY TWO NOTRUMP.

When partner opens one of a major you bid two notrump to show four trumps and a hand with at least opening bid values. Partner rebids as follows:

If he has a singleton (or void), he bids it at the three level.

If he has a good secondary suit of at least five cards, he bids it at the four level.

With no singleton or void he bids: four of his major with a minimum (12-13); three of his major with a good hand (16+); and three notrump with in between values (14-15).

Hand #1. ♠ A Q 7 6 4   ♥ 9   ♦ K J 7 5   ♣ Q 5 2

Hand #2. ♠ K J 6 5 2   ♥ J 9   ♦ K Q 7 5   ♣ Q 6

Hand #3. ♠ A K 8 6 4 3   ♥ A Q 6   ♦ K 9   ♣ J 9

In each of these examples you have opened one spade and partner has responded two notrump (Jacoby). What is your rebid?

With hand #1 you rebid three hearts to show your shortage. It is so important to locate a singleton that you are required to do this regardless of how bad your hand is.

With hand #2 you must jump to four spades to show a minimum with no singleton or void.

With hand #3 you rebid three spades to show a good hand with no singleton or void. Notice that your three-spade bid allows maximum room for slam investigation.

WARNING: When you play Jacoby Two Notrump you can not respond two notrump over a major with a balanced 10-12. Suppose partner opens one spade and you hold:

♠ 7 5   ♥ A Q 6   ♦ K 9 8 7   ♣ Q 10 6 2

If you are playing one notrump forcing in response to a major, there is no problem. Bid one notrump and plan to bid two notrump next round.

PARTNER	YOU
1♠	1NT
2♣	2NT
?	

You have now shown a balanced 10-12 and partner can decide where you belong.

Moral: Pairs who use Jacoby two notrump should also play one notrump forcing in response to a major.

The Splinter Bid

In the early sixties this author developed a convention which was described in the first edition of BID BETTER, PLAY BETTER under the heading of "THE UNUSUAL JUMP TO SHOW A SINGLETON". It proved so popular that it is now used by the vast majority of experienced players. Today it is known as the SPLINTER BID.

WEST	EAST	WEST	EAST
♠ A K 8 7 5 2	♠ J 9 6 4	1♠	4♣
♥ 8	♥ A Q 7 6	4NT	5♥
♦ K Q 7	♦ A J 8 6	6♠	Pass
♣ 8 7 4	♣ 9		

East's jump to four clubs is a splinter bid. It shows a forcing raise in spades which includes a singleton (or void) in clubs. West has no wasted values in clubs and is able to picture a slam if partner has two aces. Notice that East-West have a combined total of only 24 high-card points. Without the splinter bid it would be very difficult for them to even consider slam.

106

The chief value of the splinter bid is, of course, to get you to slam when partner has a singleton opposite your worthless holding. An additional, and very substantial benefit, however, is to keep you out of slam when partner has a singleton opposite your strength.

WEST	EAST	WEST	EAST
♠ A Q 9 8 7	♠ K J 10 5 2	1♠	4♦
♥ A	♥ K J 7	4♠	Pass
♦ K Q 7	♦ 2		
♣ J 8 6 2	♣ A 5 4 3		

This time East has shown at least four-card spade support, a hand worth 13-16, and a singleton (or void) in diamonds. West mentally tears up his king and queen of diamonds and is just able to put on the brakes.

WARNING: When responder has a singleton heart the bidding is:

WEST	EAST
1♠	4♥

This is deceptive. West might think partner had eight hearts and wished to play there. It is a good idea to discuss this exact auction with partner before you use it. Point out to him that if you really wanted to play four hearts you could bid two hearts first and then four hearts next round.

Suppose the opening bid is one heart. Four clubs and four diamonds show the singleton in a minor. With a singleton spade you bid three spades. Again this should be discussed with partner before you use it. He might think you had something like:

♠ K Q 9 8 6 5 2 ♥ 8 ♦ 8 7 4 ♣ 9 5

Point out to him that if you did have the weak hand with seven spades you would bid one spade first, then sign off in two spades and if there were another round of bidding you would sign off again in three spades.

Splinters work well in this situation:

WEST	EAST	WEST	EAST
♠ A J 10 6	♠ K Q 8 6 4	1♦	1♠
♥ A Q	♥ 9 2	4♣	4♦
♦ K Q J 9 8 7	♦ A 5 2	4♥	4NT
♣ 8	♣ J 8 5	5♥	6♠

West opens the bidding with one diamond and is delighted to hear partner respond one spade. He decides there is a game even if East has a measly six points. If he were not playing splinters he would have to bid four spades at this point, saying, "I have four trumps for you, partner, and a hand worth about 20." Playing splinters, however, he bids four clubs which is much more descriptive. It says, "I have four trumps for you, partner, and a hand worth about 20 with a singleton or void in clubs." East now bids four diamonds showing the diamond ace and slam interest. West cue-bids the heart ace and East is off to the races.

Bonus Mileage

Those who play splinters can get more mileage by agreeing that in sequences such as:

WEST	EAST
1♣	1♠
4♠	

West is denying a singleton.

For more about splinters see chapter 15.

Fourth Suit Forcing

FOURTH SUIT FORCING originated in England as a catchall bid to cover impossible bidding situations such as this:

Example 1.	WEST	EAST
	1♠	2♣
	2♥	?

108

What does East bid with the following?

♠ J 8　♥ A 8 5　♦ 6 4 2　♣ A K J 8 5

He cannot bid notrump without a diamond stopper and he should not raise partner's second suit without four-card support.

The solution is to bid three diamonds, as an ARTIFICIAL fourth suit. If East genuinely had diamonds he would be bidding some number of notrump at this point. In order for West to bid three notrump over your artificial three-diamond bid, he must have a diamond stopper.

Although the convention is commonly referred to as FOURTH SUIT FORCING, the key word here is really ARTIFICIAL. (Everyone plays this sequence forcing.)

Fourth suit forcing soon expanded to cover the problem of how responder could make a forcing jump when he was actually playing invitational jumps.

Example 2.

PARTNER (WEST)	YOU (EAST)
1♣	1♥
1♠	?

What should you bid holding:

♠ 8 2　♥ A K 8 7　♦ 8 6　♣ A Q 7 5 3

You cannot bid three clubs because it is not forcing. The solution is to use FOURTH SUIT FORCING and then bid three clubs.

In example 2. you bid two diamonds (game-forcing) and partner makes his natural rebid except that he cannot bid notrump without a diamond stopper.

Suppose the bidding continues:

PARTNER (WEST)	YOU (EAST)
1♣	1♥
1♠	2♦
2♥	3♣

Partner bids two hearts showing delayed support. You now bid three clubs which shows that you really had a forcing raise in clubs.

109

Example 3. PARTNER   YOU
              1♣   1♥
              1♠   ?

What do you bid with the following?

♠ A 8 7   ♥ A Q 10 8 4 2   ♦ 8 6   ♣ A 8

You cannot bid three hearts because it is not forcing. So you make the artificial game-force of two diamonds. Next round you will bid three hearts which has now become game-forcing.

Four-Suit Transfers Over Notrump

Many players use four-suit transfers when responding to notrump as follows:

Two diamonds shows heart length.

Two hearts shows spade length.

Two spades shows club length.

Two notrump shows diamond length.

After two spades or two notrump opener accepts the transfer with a fit for partner and makes the intermediate bid without a fit.

WARNING: When responder wishes to invite game he cannot bid two notrump directly. He has to use Stayman first even though he has no four-card major.

Four-suit transfers are not recommended for inexperienced players.

New Minor Forcing

Today most experienced players use the new minor as an artificial force over partner's rebid of one notrump.

You hold ♠ A J 8 5 3   ♥ J 7   ♦ A Q 5   ♣ J 6 4

and the auction has proceeded:

PARTNER	YOU
1♦	1♠
1NT	?

You are the captain because you know partner has a balanced 12-14. You want to play three notrump if he has only a doubleton spade but if he has three spades it is surely safer to play game in that suit. Using New Minor Forcing you bid two clubs at this point. Partner's first obligation is to show you three-card support for your major, by bidding two spades. His second obligation is to show you a four-card heart suit by bidding two hearts. Lacking either of these he will bid something else depending on his actual hand.

WARNING: Over partner's rebid of one notrump the new major is still nonforcing, unless it is a reverse.

Example:

PARTNER	YOU
1♦	1♠
1NT	2♥

Two hearts is not forcing. You have something like:

♠ K Q 8 6 5   ♥ Q J 7 5 3   ♦ 7 6   ♣ 8

Partner is supposed to pass or correct to two spades. If you had a good hand and wanted to get to game you could jump to three hearts which would be forcing.

111

Two Over One Game Forcing

Many players use 2/1 forcing to game unless responder immediately rebids the suit. Some play it forcing to game without exception.

A		B	
WEST	EAST	WEST	EAST
1♥	2♣	1♥	2♣
2♥	3♥	2♥	4♥

Playing standard, East's bid of two clubs shows ten or more points. In sequence A his raise to three hearts is encouraging but not forcing. Thus SEQUENCE B IS STRONGER THAN SEQUENCE A.

Playing 2/1 game-forcing, East's bid of two clubs is forcing to game (providing he does not immediately rebid his clubs). Therefore in Sequence A the three-heart bid is also forcing to game and leaves room for slam exploration. Notice that the four-heart bid in sequence B leaves no room below game to investigate slam. It shows that East has a minimum for his previous bidding. Thus SEQUENCE A IS STRONGER THAN SEQUENCE B.

Warning: 2/1 G.F. cannot be played without using one notrump forcing to provide for hands in the 10-12 range. It is not recommended for inexperienced players.

Inverted Minor Suit Raises

Today, many players use what are called INVERTED MINORS.

A		B	
PARTNER	YOU	PARTNER	YOU
1♦	2♦	1♦	3♦

Playing inverted minors, sequence A is forcing and shows a strong raise, (invitational or better). Sequence B is nonforcing and shows a weak raise. (Both sequences deny a four-card major.)

Playing inverted minors partner opens one diamond. What do you bid with the following?

1. ♠ 8 6 4   ♥ J 8   ♦ A Q 9 6 4   ♣ J 9 8

2. ♠ K J 8   ♥ 8 6   ♦ A Q 9 6 4   ♣ J 8 6

3. ♠ A J 8   ♥ 8 6   ♦ A Q 9 6 4   ♣ K 8 6

With hand 1. you bid three diamonds.

With hand 2. you bid two diamonds and next time you sign off in three diamonds. Partner will realize that you have a limit raise.

With hand 3. you bid two diamonds and next time you bid anything other than three diamonds. Partner will realize that you have a forcing raise.

(Reverse) Drury

When partner opens a major in third or fourth seat you will sometimes want to give him a jump raise to invite game.

<table>
<tr><td>(dealer)</td><td></td></tr>
<tr><td>YOU</td><td>PARTNER</td></tr>
<tr><td>Pass</td><td>1 ♠</td></tr>
<tr><td>?</td><td></td></tr>
</table>

You hold: ♠ K J 7   ♥ 8 6 4 2   ♦ K 10 9 8   ♣ A 6

Remember nothing is forcing by a passed hand. You are much too strong to bid two spades. For years people bid three spades to show this hand which is almost good enough to open and includes three-or four-card support. Unfortunately this could be dangerous if partner's bid was shaded and perhaps on only a four-card suit.

Then a Canadian named Drury came along and saved everyone's skin by inventing the Drury convention. He came up with the idea of using two clubs by a passed hand to show a near opening bid with three or four cards in partner's major. (Have you noticed how often the lowly two-club bid is used artificially? The strong opening two clubs, for example, or Stayman or Landy or Drury to name a few.)

Today, with the example hand, you bid two clubs after passing originally. If partner rebids two spades he is saying "For Pete's sake, pass, partner. I have a sub-minimum." And of course you pass. If partner bids anything other than two spades it means he has a genuine opening bid.

The most common sequence is:

YOU	PARTNER
Pass	1 ♠
2 ♣	4 ♠

When partner has a decent opening bid there is no point is pussyfooting around. He bids four spades.

This is not quite how Drury used the convention. He played that two diamonds by partner showed the sub-minimum. Today everyone plays two diamonds would show a real opening bid and two spades denies one which is why we call it Reverse Drury.

WARNING: If you pass originally with a club suit and partner bids one of a major you cannot bid two clubs. You will have to bid notrump or three clubs, but not two clubs.

12

The Opening Lead

In bridge the defenders always get to fire the first shot. Just as the opening salvo can affect the result of battle on the high seas, so the opening lead can affect the result of battle at the bridge table. The right lead should set the strategy for the defense and make it difficult, if not impossible, for declarer to make his contract. The wrong lead can hand it to him on a silver platter.

The problem of choosing a lead is twofold. First you must decide which suit to lead. Then you must decide which card within the suit.

Choosing the right suit can be one of the toughest problems in bridge. Choosing the correct card within the suit, however, is practically automatic. Because it is so simple we will discuss it first.

Once you have decided to attack a certain suit which card should you lead?

Of course, if you hold only one card in the suit there is no problem.

If you hold two cards in the suit it is correct to lead the higher.

Example: A̲ K A̲ 2 K̲ 3 J̲ 5 7̲ 4

With three small cards it is traditional to lead "top of nothing." (For this purpose a nine or less is considered small).

Example: 8̲ 7 2 7̲ 4 3 9̲ 7 5

However, many players prefer to lead small from three small and some lead the middle card, followed by the top card. (Middle, Up, Down, called MUD) If one of these three methods were actually superior everyone would choose it and there would no longer be three

115

different camps. As it is you simply have to agree with partner which way to play. This book will use "top of nothing."

With three to an honor it is correct to lead low, except that against a suit contract it is dangerous to lead away from an ace. You might lose it.

Against notrump: A 6 3̲ K 7 2̲ J 5 4̲ 10 5 2̲

Against a suit: A̲ 6 2 K 7 2̲ J 5 4̲ 10 5 2̲

With any three-card holding headed by two touching cards it is standard to lead the top card, except that in the United States it is traditional to lead the king from A K x.

Example: A K̲ 5 K̲ Q 2 Q̲ J 6 J̲ 10 7 9̲ 8 4

In the case of what to lead with A K x there are two schools of thought. Some lead ace and some lead king. Again it is a matter of partnership agreement. This book will use the more traditional king from ace-king.

With four or more cards it is standard to lead fourth-best unless the suit is headed by a sequence. In that case it is correct to lead top of the sequence.

Example: Q 8 6 2̲ Q 8 6 5̲ 2 Q̲ J 10 4

Against notrump a sequence needs at least three cards. (K Q 10, Q J 9, J 10 8, 10 9 7 are also considered three card sequences).

Example: Q̲ J 9 2 Q J 6 2̲ A Q 6 3̲ 2 J 9 7 5̲ 3 2

Against a suit a sequence need only be two cards long. Remember also that it is dangerous to underlead an ace against a suit contract.

Example: A̲ 8 6 4 2 K̲ Q 6 2 Q̲ J 6 2 Q 10 6 4̲ 2

116

Returning the Suit Led by Partner

When returning partner's suit, if you had three cards originally you should return the higher of your two remaining cards. If you had four (or more) cards originally you should return the card that was originally your fourth-best. (Unless you have a sequence.)

Against a notrump contract, West leads the five of hearts, an unbid suit, and the hearts are divided as follows:

```
                   DUMMY
                   ♥ 6
    WEST                          EAST
    ♥ K J 9 5 3                   ♥ A 8 2
                   DECLARER
                   ♥ Q 10 7 4
```

East wins the first trick with the ace and should return the eight, the higher of his two remaining cards. Declarer plays the ten and West wins with the jack. West knows the eight cannot be East's fourth best heart. Thus declarer has the guarded queen remaining. In order to score all five of the defense's heart tricks, West will have to wait for East to get in and lead the suit again.

Now suppose the suit is divided like this:

```
                   DUMMY
                   ♥ 6
    WEST                          EAST
    ♥ K J 9 5 3                   ♥ A 8 4 2
                   DECLARER
                   ♥ Q 10 7
```

Again West leads the heart five to East's ace. This time East returns the two, an obvious fourth-best. Declarer again plays the ten and West again wins the jack. But this time West knows he can cash all his hearts right away because declarer started with only three.

Leading the Suit that Partner Bid

There is an "old wives' tale" that says one should always lead top of partner's suit. This is incorrect. When leading partner's suit you should follow the same rules as though you were leading any other suit.

117

Example:

```
                    NORTH
                    ♠ K Q 6 2
                    ♥ A 9 6 5 3
                    ♦ 5 3 2
                    ♣ 3
WEST                                 EAST
♠ 7 4                                ♠ 8
♥ J 4 2                              ♥ Q 10 8 7
♦ K 8 4                              ♦ A J 10 9
♣ J 9 7 5 4                          ♣ A Q 6 2
                    SOUTH
                    ♠ A J 10 9 5 3
                    ♥ K
                    ♦ Q 7 6
                    ♣ K 10 8
```

EAST	SOUTH	WEST	NORTH
1♦	1♠	Pass	4♠
Pass	Pass	Pass	

Against four spades West leads his partner's suit. With three to an honor he correctly leads low to the ace. East returns the diamond jack, trapping declarer's queen, and the defenders score three diamonds and a club for down one.

Notice that if West were a believer in "old wives' tales" he would have led the diamond king originally. Now the defenders get only two diamonds and a club and declarer scores his game.

Quiz on Which Card to Lead

Against a notrump contract which card do you lead from the following holdings?

1. 10 6 2

2. A K 6 4 2

3. Q J 7 5 3 2

4. J 6

5. K Q 3

6. Q J 9 8

7. K Q 3 2

8. A 6 3 2

118

Against a suit contract which card do you lead from each of these holdings?

9. A 6 3 2   11. A K 6 3

10. K Q 6 3   12. K 4

Answers to Quiz

1. 2	7. 2
2. 4	8. 2
3. 5	9. A
4. J	10. K
5. K	11. K (or A)
6. Q	12. K

Reading Partner's Lead

When partner leads a small card the first thing to notice is how many smaller cards are missing.

Suppose South opens one notrump, North raises to three notrump and everyone passes. Partner leads the five of diamonds, clearly his fourth best, and this is what you see.

```
                    DUMMY
                    ♦ 4 2
        PARTNER                 YOU
        ♦ 5 led                 ♦ A 3
                    DECLARER
                    ?
```

You know that partner has led his smallest diamond. This means he can not have more than four cards in the suit. You have not even played to the first trick yet and you already know that declarer started with five diamonds. Unfortunately partner does not know this. Depending on the rest of your hand and the rest of dummy, it may be right for you to win the ace and shift to some other suit.

119

The Rule of Eleven

When partner leads fourth-best from a long suit you should immediately be able to tell how many cards declarer holds in his hand that are higher than the card led. A simple mechanical way to calculate this is called the rule of eleven.

Again South bids one notrump and North raises to three notrump. West leads the seven of spades and this is what you see:

```
                    DUMMY
                    ♠ K 4 3
        PARTNER                 YOU
        ♠ 7 led                 ♠ A J 9 6
                    DECLARER
                    ?
```

A small card is played from dummy. What should you play?

First try the rule of eleven. Seven from eleven is four. This means that you and dummy and declarer together have four spades higher than the seven. You can see all four of them in dummy and your hand. Therefore declarer has no spades higher than the seven.

If partner has led his fourth best, the spade layout must be:

```
                    DUMMY
                    ♠ K 4 3

        PARTNER                 YOU
        ♠ Q 10 8 7              ♠ A J 9 6
                    DECLARER
                    ♠ 5 2
```

Play the six of spades under partner's seven. This allows him to hold the lead and continue the suit. You will now win the first four tricks.

Deciding Which Suit to Attack

Next we come to the more difficult problem of deciding which suit to attack. Many texts for beginners give a list of suit combinations in

120

order of desirability with Rock of Gibraltar suggestions like ace-king-queen at the top of the list and hideous combinations like ace-queen-small at the bottom. All other things being equal one naturally should choose a suit with the safety of a good solid sequence. But rarely in bridge are all other things equal. Before leading it is important to consider carefully all that you know from the bidding as well as the thirteen cards you actually see. Good judgment is now essential and one way to develop good judgment is to study the following suggestions.

Passive Defense Versus Active Defense

There are two basic forms of defense: passive and active. In passive defense the prime object of the defenders is to play safe. They concentrate on giving nothing away by their leads and they sit back to wait for those tricks which are rightfully theirs. When a hand calls for active defense the opening leader is willing to make an aggressive and relatively dangerous lead. He often gives away a trick in order to develop two or more tricks which he might not otherwise get.

Hands which you expect to set generally call for passive defense.

SOUTH	WEST	NORTH	EAST
1 ♠	Pass	2 ♠	Pass
3 ♠	Pass	4 ♠	Pass
Pass	Pass		

As West you hold:

♠ Q J 9 5   ♥ K 4 3   ♦ 10 9 8 4 3   ♣ 8

What do you lead? Answer: The diamond ten. You should expect to set this hand. From the bidding it is clear that North-South have no extra strength in reserve. They have reached a borderline game which they might make if everything went well for them. You know, however, that declarer is in for a nasty shock in the trump suit. The bad trump break will surely spell defeat for this close contract and you should not take any unnecessary risks in leading. A heart lead might jeopardize your king while a club lead might sacrifice one of partner's tricks. Besides, there is no point in leading a singleton when you have natural trump tricks. The best lead here is the passive ten of diamonds.

121

Hands on which declarer will probably make his contract call for aggressive or attacking leads.

Example:

SOUTH	WEST	NORTH	EAST
1♥	Pass	3♦	Pass
3♥	Pass	4♥	Pass
4♠	Pass	5♣	Pass
5♥	Pass	6♥	Pass
Pass	Pass		

As West, what do you lead holding:

♠ J 8 7 6 3 2　♥ 10 9　♦ A 6　♣ K 6 3

The safest lead is the ten of hearts. But will this beat the contract? No. It does not take too much imagination to picture that dummy will look something like this:

```
                    DUMMY
                    ♠ 5
                    ♥ A 8 3
                    ♦ K Q J 10 8 5
                    ♣ A 5 4
      YOU
      ♠ J 8 7 6 3 2
      ♥ 10 9
      ♦ A 6
      ♣ K 6 3
```

If you lead a heart declarer will draw trumps then knock out your ace of diamonds. All declarer's black losers will be thrown on dummy's good diamonds and the only trick you will score is that diamond ace.

However, if you make the aggressive lead of a club and South has the club queen you have lost nothing because you had nothing to lose. But if partner has the club queen you will have struck gold.

Why not lead a spade instead of a club? It is true that dummy could have doubletons in both black suits. But if you lead a spade you will have to pray for partner to hold at least the king and queen of that suit to beat the slam. If you lead a club all partner needs is the club queen. The more modest your prayer the better the chance of its being answered.

Leading Against Notrump

Assume that South has bid one notrump and North has raised to three notrump. As West what do you lead holding:

♠ Q J 10   ♥ A Q 8 5 2   ♦ 9 6 2   ♣ J 9

Answer. Lead the heart five. The best way to develop the five tricks need to defeat the contract is to attack your longest suit. This probably gives declarer a trick he does not deserve. But when partner gets the lead he will return a heart and you hope to cash four heart tricks.

Occasionally it is better to attack partner's long suit instead of your own.
Again the bidding is one notrump-three notrump by North-South. What do you lead holding:

♠ 8 6 5 4 3 2   ♥ J 10   ♦ J 10   ♣ 9 7 2

Answer: Lead the heart jack. Here it is futile to attack spades. Even if you succeed in setting them up you have no entry to cash them. Here partner has all the entries so it is better to lead his suit which is surely hearts. North-South may well have concealed a long minor suit in the bidding. But they rarely conceal a long major.

When Should You Lead Trumps?

A trump lead is effective when declarer can be expected to ruff losers in the dummy. When declarer (or dummy) has a two-suited hand it is almost always right to lead trumps.

123

```
                    NORTH
                    ♠ 6
                    ♥ K J 9
                    ♦ A 10 8 7 5 4 2
                    ♣ J 3
        WEST                        EAST
        ♠ A 4                       ♠ J 10 9 8 5
        ♥ 6 4 2                     ♥ 5 3
        ♦ K Q J 9                   ♦ 3
        ♣ 10 9 8 7                  ♣ K Q 6 5 2
                    SOUTH
                    ♠ K Q 7 3 2
                    ♥ A Q 10 8 7
                    ♦ 7
                    ♣ A 4
```

SOUTH	WEST	NORTH	EAST
1♠	Pass	2♦	Pass
2♥	Pass	3♦	Pass
3♥	Pass	4♥	Pass
Pass	Pass		

The average West leads the diamond king here. (K Q J 9 is high on that text-book list of desirable opening leads.) Look what happens. Declarer wins the diamond ace and leads a spade to the king and ace. West now realizes that there is no future in diamonds and he tries the club ten. South wins the club ace, cashes the spade queen and crossruffs to make an overtrick.

If West had listened to the bidding he would have led a heart originally. Then when he won the spade ace he would lead another heart. Now declarer can ruff only one spade and the contract must fail. Try it.

Against Six Notrump or Any Grand Slam
Make the Safest Lead in Your Hand

Try this one:

SOUTH	WEST	NORTH	EAST
2♣	Pass	2♦	Pass
2♠	Pass	3♠	Pass
4NT	Pass	5♦	Pass
7♠	Pass	Pass	Pass

124

What do you lead, as West, with this magnificent collection:

♠ 9 4 2   ♥ 9 4 2   ♦ 9 4 2   ♣ 9 6 4 2

Life may look pretty grim at the moment but keep a stiff upper lip and you may beat this hand yet. Declarer could be missing a queen somewhere for which he has a two-way finesse. He may misguess provided you do not let the cat out of the bag by leading that suit. Which queen does partner hold? You do not know. But you do know from the bidding that your side is not going to win any trump tricks. If partner has the trump queen it is a singleton anyway. The safest lead here is a trump.

When Should You Lead a Singleton?

A singleton is a very aggressive and potentially dangerous lead because it can damage your partner's hand severely. Yet the average player eagerly throws his singleton on the table without any forethought as to what it may accomplish. Here is an extreme example:

```
                    NORTH
                    ♠ J 8 6 5
                    ♥ A J 10
                    ♦ J 8 4 3
                    ♣ A 2
    WEST                            EAST
    ♠ A 4 3                         ♠ 2
    ♥ Q 9 8 5 4                     ♥ 6 3 2
    ♦ 9                             ♦ K 10 6 2
    ♣ J 10 9 6                      ♣ 8 7 5 4 3
                    SOUTH
                    ♠ K Q 10 9 7
                    ♥ K 7
                    ♦ A Q 7 5
                    ♦ K Q
```

SOUTH	WEST	NORTH	EAST
1 ♠	Pass	3 ♠	Pass
4NT	Pass	5 ♥	Pass
6 ♠	Pass	Pass	Pass

125

West led the singleton diamond, dummy covered, and South topped East's king with the ace. After drawing trumps declarer led the diamond eight from dummy and easily brought home the whole suit. With the normal lead of the club jack, South would probably have misguessed the diamond situation and gone down.

The saddest part is that West had absolutely nothing to gain by the lead. If East had an entry it would mean that the contract was down already, thanks to West's ace of trumps.

Suppose, however, that West had the same hand but with three little trumps instead of A 4 3. Now the singleton lead has much to recommend it. This time East figures to have one ace. If it is the ace of diamonds or the ace of spades he will be able to give West a diamond ruff to beat the contract.

Against a game contract, the ideal time to lead a singleton is when you hold a trump entry plus an EXTRA trump to ruff with, such as K x x or A x. A singleton lead is less effective with a trump holding of Q x x or K x because you may find yourself ruffing with a natural trump trick.

While we are on the subject of singletons, do not forget that it can be a good idea to lead partner's singleton.

SOUTH	WEST	NORTH	EAST
1 ♠	Pass	2 ♦	Pass
4 ♦	Pass	4 ♠	Pass
6 ♠	Pass	Pass	Pass

What should West lead holding:

♠ A 4   ♥ 8 7 6 2   ♦ 9 6 4 3   ♣ Q J 10

Answer: Lead a diamond. Then grab the trump ace at the first possible moment and lead another diamond for partner to ruff.

When Defender Holds Long Trumps

A singleton is usually a poor lead when defender has long trumps — four or more. In this case it is probably better to force declarer by leading your own suit.

126

```
                    NORTH
                    ♠ 6 4 2
                    ♥ Q 10
                    ♦ J 7 5 3
                    ♣ A K Q J
        WEST                      EAST
        ♠ A 8 7 5                 ♠ 3
        ♥ 4                       ♥ A 7 6 5 3 2
        ♦ A Q 9 8 4               ♦ K 10 6 2
        ♣ 4 3 2                   ♣ 8 5
                    SOUTH
                    ♠ K Q J 10 9
                    ♥ K J 9 8
                    ♦ —
                    ♣ 10 9 7 6
```

NORTH	EAST	SOUTH	WEST
1♣	Pass	1♠	Pass
1NT	Pass	3♥	Pass
3♠	Pass	4♠	Pass
Pass	Pass		

At first it looks as though declarer has only two losers in four spades: the spade ace and the heart ace. If West leads a heart he will get one ruff and declarer makes ten tricks. But if West starts with the diamond ace and the defense continue with diamonds at every logical opportunity, declarer can never make even ten tricks. Try it.

Is It Better to Lead Your Suit or Partner's

There are naturally many factors involved in making the right decision: your holding in partner's suit: the circumstances under which partner bid; the texture of your own suit, and so on. If you are still in doubt after weighing all the evidence, I suggest that you lead partner's suit. The reason is this: If you lead your own suit and it turns out to be wrong, partner, being only human, is going to be annoyed that you did not lead his suit. However, if you do lead his suit and that turns out to be wrong he will be relatively understanding. At least you will have preserved partnership harmony.

127

Lead-Directing Doubles

Sometimes a defender will have the opportunity to make a lead-directing double. A double of an artificial bid is the most common.

SOUTH	WEST	NORTH	EAST
1NT	Pass	2♣	Dbl.
2♠	Pass	3NT	Pass
Pass	Pass		

If two clubs were a natural bid, East's double would be for take-out. Here North's bid of two clubs is artificial, asking for a major. East's double is therefore for penalties and shows a hand something like:

♠ A 6 5   ♥ 8 6 5   ♦ 8 2   ♣ K Q J 9 7

Against three notrump West will lead a club which may well defeat the contract.

The Double of Three Notrump is Lead-Directing

Example 1.

EAST	SOUTH	WEST	NORTH
1♦	1NT	Pass	3NT
Dbl.	Pass	Pass	Pass

East is doubling to ensure that he gets a diamond lead. Without the double West might be tempted to experiment with another suit, particularly if he has only a singleton diamond. The double says "Lead my suit, partner and I have the contract beaten in my own hand."

Example 2.

SOUTH	WEST	NORTH	EAST
1♣	1♥	1♠	Pass
1NT	Pass	3NT	Dbl.
Pass	Pass	Pass	

This time East wants partner to lead his own suit, hearts. East probably has a heart honor plus other defense.

128

Example 3.

SOUTH	WEST	NORTH	EAST
1♦	Pass	1♥	Pass
2NT	Pass	3NT	Dbl.
Pass	Pass	Pass	

When the defenders have never bid, the double of three notrump calls for the lead of dummy's suit. Here East is loaded in hearts.

The Lightner Slam Double

A double of a voluntarily bid slam is lead-directing. Known as the Lightner Slam Double after its inventor, it calls for an UNUSUAL lead, never trumps and never the suit that you would normally be expected to lead if there had been no double.

Example 1.

EAST	SOUTH	WEST	NORTH
1♠	2♥	Pass	6♥
Dbl.	Pass	Pass	Pass

If East had not doubled West would be expected to lead a spade. By doubling, East is desperately asking West NOT to lead a spade. East is probably void in either clubs or diamonds and West should be able to tell which by looking at his own distribution.

Warning: If East expects the contract to fail with a plain old ordinary spade lead he must not double.

Example 2.

SOUTH	WEST	NORTH	EAST
1♠	Pass	2♣	Pass
3♠	Pass	6♠	Dbl.
Pass	Pass	Pass	

If East had not doubled, West would probably lead a red suit. The double here asks for dummy's suit. East could be void in clubs.

129

Quiz on Opening Leads

Warning! Just because you have read this chapter carefully does not mean that you can sit back and relax and do well on this quiz. This is a tough quiz. If you get more than half the questions right you have done well. If you get them all right I shall expect to see you in the finals of next year's Blue Ribbon pairs.

Remember, no one can teach you what to lead on every hand. You must develop the habit of picturing all four hands and thinking for yourself.

In each of the following problems you are West. What should you lead and why?

1.

SOUTH	WEST	NORTH	EAST
1 ♦	Dbl.	Pass	Pass
Pass			

You hold:

♠ A Q 6 2   ♥ Q J 10 7   ♦ 4   ♣ K Q 10 4

2.

SOUTH	WEST	NORTH	EAST
1 ♣	Pass	3 ♣	Pass
3 ♦	Pass	3 ♠	Pass
4 ♣	Pass	5 ♣	Pass
Pass	Pass		

You hold:

♠ K 9 5 3   ♥ A Q 4 3   ♦ J 10 8   ♣ 8 7

3.

SOUTH	WEST	NORTH	EAST
1 ♠	Pass	3 ♠	Pass
7 ♠	Pass	Pass	Pass

You hold:

♠ 2   ♥ J 6 2   ♦ J 6 5 2   ♣ J 6 5 4 2

4.

SOUTH	WEST	NORTH	EAST
1♥	Pass	1NT	Pass
2♦	Pass	3♦	Pass
Pass	Pass		

You hold:

♠ A Q 5   ♥ J   ♦ J 6 4 3 2   ♣ K 10 5 4

5.

SOUTH	WEST	NORTH	EAST
1NT	Pass	3NT	Pass
Pass	Pass		

You hold:

♠ A Q 8 6 4   ♥ J 10 9 8   ♥ 8 7   ♣ 7 6

6.

SOUTH	WEST	NORTH	EAST
2NT	Pass	Pass	Pass

You hold:

♠ 10 9 2   ♥ K J 6 2   ♦ Q 7 3 2   ♣ 4 3

7.

NORTH	EAST	SOUTH	WEST
1NT	2♥	3♠	Pass
4♠	Pass	6♠	Pass
Pass	Dbl.	Pass	Pass
Pass			

You hold:

♠ 10 2   ♥ J 10   ♦ Q 9 6 4 3 2   ♣ J 10 9

8.

SOUTH	WEST	NORTH	EAST
1NT	Pass	3NT	Dbl.
Pass	Pass	Pass	

You hold:

♠ 10 9 7 5   ♥ 7   ♦ 9 7 5 2   ♣ J 6 4 2

Answers to Quiz

1. The diamond four. Picture partner's hand. Your double asked him to choose between spades, hearts and clubs. If he does not have four cards in one of those suits he may have to bid a three-card suit. But partner has decided to overrule you. Why? Because his diamonds are better than South's diamonds. In fact East expects to score more defending one diamond doubled than anywhere else.

    Now look at it from declarer's point of view. In addition to the high cards in his hand he has several little diamonds with which he is hoping to win tricks by ruffing, To stop him from doing this the defenders must draw trumps fast. When partner leaves in your double of a one-bid he is hoping for a trump lead.

2. The heart ace. Did you hear anybody bid notrump? North-South passed the ball back and forth for quite a while, each trying to get the other fellow to bid notrump. They know it is easier to make nine tricks at notrump than eleven in a minor. But nobody bid notrump because nobody had a heart stopper. Lead the heart ace and cash as many hearts as you can before they run away.

3. The club four. Against any grand slam you should make the safest lead in your hand. The singleton trump is dangerous because partner just might hold Q x x. The heart, diamond and club leads are also risky as they may be setting up declarer's side suit. The club lead is the least risky because you have so many it is unlikely that either opponent has four of them.

4. Lead a trump and plan to lead another trump every time you get a chance. North and South each have four diamonds. They can make eight tricks by crossruffing alone if trumps are never led. Each time you lead a trump you hold declarer to one less trick.

5. The spade six. Hearts may be safer but you have more chance of defeating the contract by leading a spade.

6. The spade ten. You should expect to beat this contract. With no entries to dummy, declarer is going to have trouble. Do not make a risky lead.

7. The diamond four. Partner is calling for an unusual lead, not hearts and not trumps. He is probably void in diamonds.

8. The heart seven. This is a lead directing double. It says "lead my suit, partner, and I will beat this contract." The only problem is that East never got a chance to bid his suit. Fortunately you can tell from your own hand that it is hearts.

Whether or not you did well on this quiz is unimportant, because the questions were only partially based on the material in the chapter. The primary object of the quiz was to introduce some fresh ideas on opening leads. While you were reading the answers were you able to say, even once, "Well I never considered that angle before." If so the quiz was a success and you are that much better equipped to fire the opening salvo of the defense.

13

The Art of Signaling

Ever since Lord Henry Bentinck first invented the high-low signal in 1834, experienced players have been using their "immaterial" cards to send messages back and forth across the table. Take the following example:

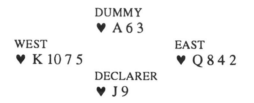

```
                 DUMMY
                 ♥ A 6 3
   WEST                      EAST
   ♥ K 10 7 5                ♥ Q 8 4 2
                 DECLARER
                 ♥ J 9
```

Against a notrump contract West leads the heart five. If a low card is played from dummy, East naturally plays the queen in an attempt to win the trick. If dummy puts up the ace, however, East has a choice of three relatively "immaterial" cards to play: the eight, the four, or the two. A beginner would probably play the two simply because it was his smallest card. At any rate no special meaning should be attached to his choice. An experienced player would play the eight as a signal to partner that he wanted the suit continued.

Today a signal can convey any one of three separate messages depending on the situation in which it is used.

The three available signals are:

1. The attitude signal.
2. The count signal.
3. The suit-preference signal.

Although the student soon learns to use these signals, he is rarely taught which signal applies when. Consequently, he uses them all indiscriminately. By the time he has become a fairly sophisticated player in other respects his defense is a complete hodge-podge. Even among very good players one often hears remarks like these.

First player: "Why didn't you continue hearts, partner? I gave you the ten!"

Partner: "It looked like a suit-preference signal to me. I thought you wanted a spade shift."

Or

First player: "Why did you give me that come-on signal in clubs?"

Partner: "That was no come-on signal! I was just trying to give you the count."

What is the solution to all this confusion? A simple bit of old-fashioned organization. Let us start at the beginning.

The Attitude Signal

The first signal a beginner learns is the attitude signal, (often called the come-on signal). The principle is this: When your partner leads a suit and you have the opportunity to signal, you normally play a high card if you want the suit continued and a low card if you do not want the suit continued.

Example 1.

NORTH
♠ K 6 2
♥ 10 7
♦ K 10 9 7 2
♣ A 8 4

WEST
♠ 10 9 7
♥ A K 5
♦ 8 6 4
♣ J 9 6 3

EAST
♠ J 8 4 3
♥ Q 8 6 4 2
♦ 5 3
♣ Q 10

SOUTH
♠ A Q 5
♥ J 9 3
♦ A Q J
♣ K 7 6 2

SOUTH	WEST	NORTH	EAST
1NT	Pass	3NT	Pass
Pass	Pass		

135

Against three notrump West leads the heart king. East is delighted and should play the eight to encourage partner to continue. Actually East has four gradations of signal available, the eight, six, four or two. Here are the approximate meanings of each:

The two: "Stop leading hearts."
The four: "I can tolerate a heart continuation."
The six: "Please continue hearts."
The eight: "WHOOPEE! YOU'VE HIT THE JACKPOT!"

Partner is not always able to distinguish between slight gradations of signal, so when you are sure that you want something, SHOUT! Do not whisper.

Example 2.

```
                        NORTH
                        ♠ Q 10 5 4
                        ♥ J 5 4 3
                        ♦ Q J 6
                        ♣ K Q
        WEST                            EAST
        ♠ A K 7 2                       ♠ 8 3
        ♥ 10 2                          ♥ 9 7
        ♦ 10 9 7                        ♦ 8 5 4 2
        ♣ 5 4 3 2                       ♣ A J 8 7 6
                        SOUTH
                        ♠ J 9 6
                        ♥ A K Q 8 6
                        ♦ A K 3
                        ♣ 10 9
```

SOUTH	WEST	NORTH	EAST
1♥	Pass	3♥	Pass
4♥	Pass	Pass	Pass

Against four hearts West leads the spade king on which East should play the eight, because he wants the suit continued. West obediently continues with the ace and another spade for East to ruff. The ace of clubs now sets the contract. If East-West fail to get their spade ruff declarer will make his game.

Notice that in both examples the attitude signal applied because the signaler's partner led to the trick involved.

A Discard Can Also Be An Attitude Signal

Example 3.

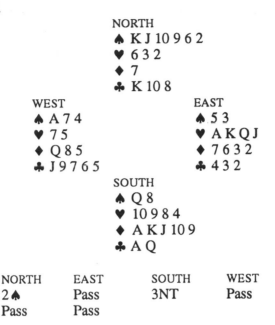

NORTH
♠ K J 10 9 6 2
♥ 6 3 2
♦ 7
♣ K 10 8

WEST
♠ A 7 4
♥ 7 5
♦ Q 8 5
♣ J 9 7 6 5

EAST
♠ 5 3
♥ A K Q J
♦ 7 6 3 2
♣ 4 3 2

SOUTH
♠ Q 8
♥ 10 9 8 4
♦ A K J 10 9
♣ A Q

NORTH	EAST	SOUTH	WEST
2♠	Pass	3NT	Pass
Pass	Pass		

Against three notrump West leads the club six. Dummy plays the eight, East plays the two showing no interest in clubs, and South's ace wins the trick. Declarer now attacks spades and West holds off until the third round, giving partner a chance to signal. East is desperate for a heart shift but he can not spare one to signal with. He needs four heart tricks to set the contract. The best he can do is to throw the two of diamonds, a negative signal meaning, "Don't lead diamonds." If West is alert, he will switch to a heart and declarer will be down one.

The Count Signal

When declarer (or dummy) leads a suit, the attitude signal becomes relatively useless. After all, if declarer is voluntarily attacking a suit it is hardly likely that a defender also wants to attack it. Confucius say, "Two teams attack same suit, one team need spectacles." Therefore, when declarer leads a suit it has been found much more valuable to give count rather than attitude.

The general rule is this: When declarer leads a plain suit (any suit except trump), a defender will echo (play high-low) to indicate that he holds an even number of cards in that suit. And he will play his lowest card first to indicate that he holds an odd number of cards in the suit.

If you have difficulty remembering this:

Play HIGH with EVEN. (Two 4-letter words).

Play LOW with ODD. (Two 3-letter words).

Here is a typical example.

Example 4.

```
                    NORTH
                    ♠ 8 5 4
                    ♥ 6 5
                    ♦ 4 3 2
                    ♣ K Q J 10 5
        WEST                        EAST
        ♠ 10 9 7                    ♠ 6 3 2
        ♥ K 10 8 7 3                ♥ J 9
        ♦ Q 5                       ♦ K J 8 7 6
        ♣ 9 3 2                     ♣ A 7 4
                    SOUTH
                    ♠ A K Q J
                    ♥ A Q 4 2
                    ♦ A 10 9
                    ♣ 8 6
```

SOUTH	WEST	NORTH	EAST
2NT	Pass	3NT	Pass
Pass	Pass		

Against three notrump West leads the heart seven. South wins East's jack with the queen and leads a club. The result here is going to depend on when the ace of clubs is played. Suppose East wins the first round of clubs and returns a heart. Declarer will score two heart tricks, four spades, four clubs and one diamond for a total of eleven tricks. Now suppose East holds up his ace twice and wins the third round. This time declarer makes only two club tricks, four spades, two hearts and one diamond for a total of nine tricks. Even better, from the defenders point of view, is for East to hold up his ace exactly once and win the second round of clubs. Now declarer can make only one club trick for a total of just eight tricks and he is down one.

The point is that East does best to take his ace on the same trick that declarer plays his last club. If declarer has two clubs East must win the second round. And if declarer has three clubs East must win the third round. Of course, South is not planning to tell anyone how many clubs he has. But if West is an experienced player he will indicate whether he has an odd number of clubs or an even number. As the cards lie he will play his lowest club, the two, to show an odd number. Once West is known to hold an odd number of clubs East has no trouble placing the notrump bidder with a doubleton. He holds up exactly once and defeats the contract.

The count signal can be just as important against a suit contract.

Example 5.

NORTH
♠ 6 5 4
♥ K Q J 2
♦ Q 6 2
♣ 10 8 2

WEST
♠ J 3
♥ 6 5 4 3
♦ 10 8 5 3
♣ K J 5

EAST
♠ 10 2
♥ A 10 9
♦ K J 9 4
♣ Q 9 7 6

SOUTH
♠ A K Q 9 8 7
♥ 8 7
♦ A 7
♣ A 4 3

SOUTH	WEST	NORTH	EAST
1 ♠	Pass	2 ♠	Pass
4 ♠	Pass	Pass	Pass

139

West leads the three of diamonds covered by the queen, king and ace. Declarer draws trump and leads the heart eight to the king. Your average East grabs this with the ace and tries to cash as many diamonds as he can. West, by the way, forgot all about playing high to indicate an even number of hearts, but it did not matter because East was not watching anyway. South ruffs the third round of diamonds and scores six spades, two hearts and two minor suit aces to make his game.

Now suppose East and West are experienced players. When the first heart is led West will play the six, the highest card that he can afford, to show an even number of hearts. Note that East has no trouble reading this. The six cannot be West's lowest heart. East works out that declarer has either two or four hearts. He can do nothing about four hearts, so he concentrates on defending against a doubleton heart in declarer's hand. Accordingly, he ducks the first heart lead and wins the second. This cuts declarer off from dummy. South scores only one heart trick and the contract fails.

The Trump Echo

In the trump suit the count signal is reversed. Following to trumps a defender plays high-low to indicate an odd number and plays up the line to indicate an even number.

This seems strange at first until you consider the evolution of the signal. All signals were originally attention-getters. Playing high-low in trumps was first used to alert partner to a third trump and a desire to ruff something.

Example 6.

NORTH
♠ Q 6 5 4
♥ K 6 4 2
♦ 8 5 4
♣ A 2

WEST
♠ 8 7 3
♥ 3
♦ J 7 6 3 2
♣ 10 9 6 5

EAST
♠ A
♥ A 10 9 7 5
♦ K Q 10 9
♣ 8 7 4

SOUTH
♠ K J 10 9 2
♥ Q J 8
♦ A
♣ K Q J 3

EAST	SOUTH	WEST	NORTH
1♥	1♠	Pass	2♠
Pass	4♠	Pass	Pass
Pass			

Against four spades West leads his singleton heart. East wins the ace and returns the heart ten which West trumps with the eight-spot. West now leads the diamond three to the queen and ace. Declarer leads a spade to the queen on which West contributes the three and East wins with the ace. At this point the defenders need one more trick to set the contract. Should East try to cash the diamond king or should he try to give partner another heart ruff?. He is not sure that South has another diamond, but he knows from the trump echo that partner has another spade. Accordingly, he leads a third heart and the contract is down one.

The Suit-Preference Signal

The suit-preference signal occurs most often where a ruff is involved.

Example 7.

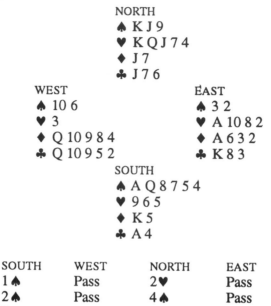

NORTH
♠ K J 9
♥ K Q J 7 4
♦ J 7
♣ J 7 6

WEST
♠ 10 6
♥ 3
♦ Q 10 9 8 4
♣ Q 10 9 5 2

EAST
♠ 3 2
♥ A 10 8 2
♦ A 6 3 2
♣ K 8 3

SOUTH
♠ A Q 8 7 5 4
♥ 9 6 5
♦ K 5
♣ A 4

SOUTH	WEST	NORTH	EAST
1 ♠	Pass	2 ♥	Pass
2 ♠	Pass	4 ♠	Pass
Pass	Pass		

Against four spades West leads the heart three and East has no difficulty recognizing that this is a singleton. He wins the ace and carefully returns the ten of hearts, a HIGH card to indicate an entry in the HIGHER-ranking of the two side suits. (For the purposes of suit preference the trump suit is ignored.)

West ruffs this and returns a diamond to the ace. East gives him a second heart ruff to defeat the contract.

Note that if East had held the club ace instead of the diamond ace he would have returned the heart two at the second trick. A HIGH card asks for the HIGHER-ranking suit. A LOW card asks for the LOWER-ranking suit.

Here is another example of suit preference at work:

Example 8.

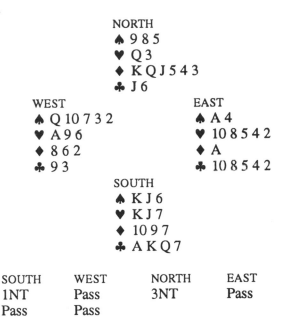

NORTH
♠ 9 8 5
♥ Q 3
♦ K Q J 5 4 3
♣ J 6

WEST
♠ Q 10 7 3 2
♥ A 9 6
♦ 8 6 2
♣ 9 3

EAST
♠ A 4
♥ 10 8 5 4 2
♦ A
♣ 10 8 5 4 2

SOUTH
♠ K J 6
♥ K J 7
♦ 10 9 7
♣ A K Q 7

SOUTH	WEST	NORTH	EAST
1NT	Pass	3NT	Pass
Pass	Pass		

Against three notrump West leads the spade three. East wins the ace and returns the four. South puts in the jack which loses to the queen. At this point West can knock out declarer's king with any one of his three remaining spades: the ten, the seven, or the two. He should select the ten, his highest spade, so that when East wins his ace of diamonds he will return a heart, the higher-ranking of the two possible suits where West could hold an entry.

Without the suit-preference signal, East would face a complete guess as to whether to return a club or a heart. Thanks to suit-preference East returns a heart and the contract is down two.

The suit-preference signal is used most frequently in belated lead situations like the two examples just given. It can occasionally apply on opening lead providing it can not possibly be interpreted as a normal fourth-best.

Example 9.

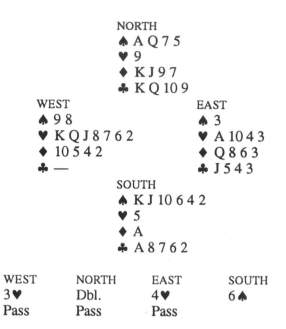

```
                     NORTH
                     ♠ A Q 7 5
                     ♥ 9
                     ♦ K J 9 7
                     ♣ K Q 10 9
        WEST                        EAST
        ♠ 9 8                       ♠ 3
        ♥ K Q J 8 7 6 2             ♥ A 10 4 3
        ♦ 10 5 4 2                  ♦ Q 8 6 3
        ♣ —                         ♣ J 5 4 3
                     SOUTH
                     ♠ K J 10 6 4 2
                     ♥ 5
                     ♦ A
                     ♣ A 8 7 6 2
```

WEST	NORTH	EAST	SOUTH
3♥	Dbl.	4♥	6♠
Pass	Pass	Pass	

West leads the heart two. Under normal circumstances this would probably be fourth-best from a four-card suit. In view of West's opening bid, however, this is obviously impossible. East correctly interprets the heart two as a suit-preference signal calling for the lower-ranking side-suit. He wins the heart ace and returns a club to set the slam.

Signaling With an Honor

When you signal with a high honor (the ace, king or queen), you promise the honor just below it and deny the honor just above. This is usually (but not always) true when the jack or ten is used as a signal.

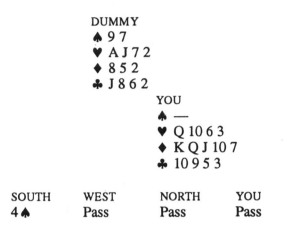

DUMMY
♠ 9 7
♥ A J 7 2
♦ 8 5 2
♣ J 8 6 2

YOU
♠ —
♥ Q 10 6 3
♦ K Q J 10 7
♣ 10 9 5 3

SOUTH	WEST	NORTH	YOU
4 ♠	Pass	Pass	Pass

Partner leads the club king against four spades. South ruffs this and leads the ace of spades. What do you throw?

You should throw the king of diamonds. Not only do you promise great diamonds but you guarantee the queen and deny the ace, all of which may be very helpful to partner.

145

Example 10.

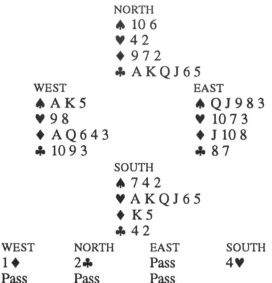

NORTH
♠ 10 6
♥ 4 2
♦ 9 7 2
♣ A K Q J 6 5

WEST
♠ A K 5
♥ 9 8
♦ A Q 6 4 3
♣ 10 9 3

EAST
♠ Q J 9 8 3
♥ 10 7 3
♦ J 10 8
♣ 8 7

SOUTH
♠ 7 4 2
♥ A K Q J 6 5
♦ K 5
♣ 4 2

WEST	NORTH	EAST	SOUTH
1♦	2♣	Pass	4♥
Pass	Pass	Pass	

West leads the spade king against four hearts and East helpfully signals with the queen. West is now able to lead the spade five to partner's jack and a diamond return sinks the contract.

Warning: Suppose the lay-out is:

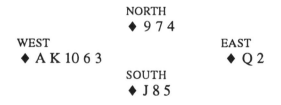

NORTH
♦ 9 7 4

WEST
♦ A K 10 6 3

EAST
♦ Q 2

SOUTH
♦ J 8 5

Against a major suit game West leads the diamond king and East is anxious to ruff the third round. He must NOT play the queen on the first trick to indicate a doubleton, because West might then underlead his ace trusting East to have the jack as in example 10.

In most cases West will work out the situation for himself. Here he will continue with the ace and when East's queen drops he will give partner a third-round ruff.

146

Quiz on Signaling

Problem 1.

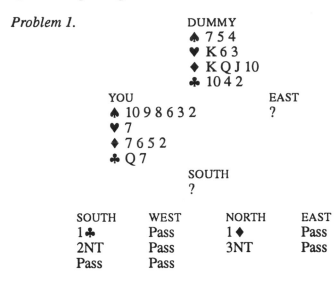

DUMMY
♠ 7 5 4
♥ K 6 3
♦ K Q J 10
♣ 10 4 2

YOU
♠ 10 9 8 6 3 2
♥ 7
♦ 7 6 5 2
♣ Q 7

EAST
?

SOUTH
?

SOUTH	WEST	NORTH	EAST
1♣	Pass	1♦	Pass
2NT	Pass	3NT	Pass
Pass	Pass		

Against three notrump you lead the spade ten and partner plays the queen. Declarer wins the ace and leads a diamond at trick two. Which diamond do you play?

Problem 2.

DUMMY
♠ Q J 10
♥ K 7 4 2
♦ A Q
♣ K Q J 9

WEST
?

YOU
♠ 8 3
♥ Q J 10
♦ K J 8 7 5
♣ 8 5 2

SOUTH
?

NORTH	EAST	SOUTH	WEST
1♣	Pass	1♥	Pass
3♥	Pass	4♥	Pass
Pass	Pass		

Against four hearts partner leads the spade king. Which spade do you play?

147

Problem 3.

```
                    DUMMY
                    ♠ Q J 5 3
                    ♥ A 9 8 4
                    ♦ 8 5
                    ♣ 8 4 2
        YOU                         EAST
        ♠ A K 7 2                   ?
        ♥ 6
        ♦ 9 7 6 2
        ♣ A J 10 2
                    SOUTH
                    ?
```

SOUTH	WEST	NORTH	EAST
1♥	Pass	3♥	Pass
Pass	Pass		

Against three hearts you lead the spade king and partner drops the nine. You continue with the spade ace and partner plays the four. What card do you lead next?

Answers to Quiz

1. Play the diamond seven, a high card to let partner know that you have an even number of cards in the suit.

2. Play the spade three. You do not want partner to continue spades and give you a ruff because you have a natural trump trick. You really want partner to switch to a diamond. You plan to beat this contract with the diamond king, one trump trick and two spades. Unless partner shifts to a diamond right now, however, you may never get the king. When you discourage in spades he will work out from the appearance of dummy that the most helpful switch is to a diamond.

3. Lead the spade two, a suit-preference signal. Partner will ruff the third spade and return a club, the lower ranking of the two plausible suits.

148

14

Two Tough Nuts to Crack

This chapter will explore and attempt to simplify two areas of bridge that are generally considered very complicated. These are the *PROBABILITIES OF DISTRIBUTION* and the theory of *RESTRICTED CHOICE*. You can play an excellent game of bridge without understanding either of them, but you will never quite *FEEL* like an expert. A working acquaintance with these two areas, however, will not only increase your chances of making certain contracts, it will also cause you to appear superior in the eyes of your fellow players.

When we talk about the probabilities of distribution, we get into the field of mathematics and many people immediately become gunshy. Do not let it bother you. To be a top-flight player, all you need to know about mathematics is how to count up to thirteen. Any more advanced calculation has already been worked out for you by the mathematicians. Good players become familiar with these play combinations, because even for a mathematician it would be far too tedious to work everything out at the table. Mathematicians have no special advantage at the table, and sometimes make very poor players.

Where the mathematician really shines is at the party after the game. Here he can always impress his fellow bridge addicts with solutions to various percentage problems. Take the problem of the two red kings:

149

Problem 1.

NORTH
♠ 6 4
♥ A Q J 6
♦ A Q J 4
♣ K 5 3

WEST   EAST
?   ?

SOUTH
♠ A K 8 2
♥ 10 9 3
♦ 10 9 2
♣ A Q J

You are South and find yourself in a contract of six notrump. Before a card has been touched, what are your chances of making the slam? Obviously the only way to play the hand is to take repeated finesses in hearts and diamond. You won't be defeated unless East holds both red kings.

What are your chances? Most good bridge players will say 75% After all, East will have the heart king half the time. And half the time that he has the heart king he will also have the diamond king. Half of a half is a quarter. So you will lose one quarter, or 25% of the time, and make your slam 75% of the time.

This is only approximately correct. As the mathematician is happy to inform you, the exact chance of success is 76 percent.

You want him to explain this? First he gets out paper and pencil and puts a most intelligent expression on his face. Then he proceeds to write out a mathematical formula that somehow reminds you of Einstein's theory of relativity. By this time you are sorry you asked and are thoroughly bored by the whole subject.

Don't blame the mathematician too severely. He is a victim of the system he was taught, whereby an extremely simple problem is handled as abstrusely as an advanced calculus equation.

Actually the problem is so simple that a ten-year-old should be able to solve it easily without paper or pencil *PROVIDED THAT IT IS EXPLAINED TO HIM VISUALLY.*

If you have no sense of humor and prefer to deal with life ponderously and profoundly, I suggest that you skip the rest of this chapter. If you're still with me, however, I think you will agree that this type of problem can be fun. So erase that worried look and let's go!

First, imagine a round wooden tray with twenty-six holes in it. Now mentally draw a line down the center of the tray so that there are thirteen holes on the left of the line and thirteen on the right.

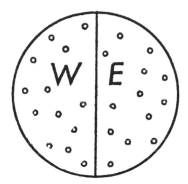

Assume that the tray is so constructed that a marble falling onto it will eventually come to rest in one of the holes. It cannot roll off the tray because there is a railing around the edge. The holes are laid out in such a way that a marble has an equal chance of coming to rest in any one of them.

The thirteen holes on the left of the line represent West's thirteen cards, and the thirteen holes on the right represent East's. Now let us take two imaginary red marbles to represent the two red kings. The act of dropping the marbles determines the fate of the deal. (The other 24 cards in the East-West hands are irrelevant.)

Now we are ready to drop the first marble. What are the chances of East getting it?

East has 13 holes and there are twenty-six hold altogether, so East's chances are thirteen out of twenty-six, or *ONE HALF.* Now suppose that East gets the first marble. What are his chances of also getting the second?

There are only twelve holes remaining on the East side because one is filled up by the first marble. And there are only twenty-five holes left on the entire tray, so East's chances of getting the second marble are twelve out of twenty-five or 12/25. Since his chance of getting the first was one-half, his chance of getting BOTH is one half of 12/25. That is 6/25, or 24%.

So you will be defeated 24% of the time, and make your slam 76% of the time. Give this problem to your bridge expert friends. You'll be surprised how few of them will know the answer.

You can use the same wooden tray to figure out any distribution problem. Let's try something a little harder this time.

Suppose the trump suit is divided between your hand and dummy as follows:

Problem 2.

```
              NORTH (DUMMY)
              9 8 7 6
WEST                          EAST
?                             ?
              SOUTH (YOU)
              A K 10 5 4
```

Before any card has been played, what are the chances that West will have the doubleton queen-jack of trumps?

Get out the wooden tray and four marbles this time, to represent the four missing trumps: queen, jack, three and two. Now let's have a look.

We'll drop the queen first, although it makes no difference what order is used. Her chances of going to West are 13/26. Now the jack. His chances of going to West are 12/25. Next drop the three. Remember, If West is going to get the queen-jack alone, the three and the two must go to East. East's chances of getting the three are 13/24, since there are thirteen holes still open in the East hand and only twenty-four holes open on the entire tray. And finally East's chances of getting the two are 12/23. So the chance that West will have the queen-jack of trumps and East the three-two are:

$$\frac{13}{26} \times \frac{12}{25} \times \frac{13}{24} \times \frac{12}{23}$$

which comes to 6.78%

Because we used four marbles this time there was more multiplication involved. Unfortunately, the multiplication becomes more tedious the more marbles we use.

Now that you know how to figure the chances of any particular distribution occurring, here is a handy table of the more common distributions to save you the trouble.

Distribution of Cards in Two Unknown Hands

Cards Outstanding in a Suit	Division	Percent Probability
2	1-1	52.00
	2-0	48.00
3	2-1	78.00
	3-0	22.00
4	3-1	49.74
	2-2	40.70
	4-0	9.57
5	3-2	67.83
	4-1	28.26
	5-0	3.91
6	4-2	48.45
	3-3	35.53
	5-1	14.53
	6-0	1.49
7	4-3	62.17
	5-2	30.52
	6-1	6.78
	7-0	0.52
8	5-3	47.12
	4-4	32.72
	6-2	17.14
	7-1	2.86
	8-0	0.16

Do not try to memorize this table. Do notice, however, that an odd number of cards tends to break as evenly as possible but an even number does not. Thus if you are missing five spades you can expect them to break three-two. But if you are missing six spades they probably will not break three-three.

Instead of using the wooden tray for problem 2, for example, we could simply have checked the 2-2 division in the table where we find

153

that four cards will produce a 2-2 split 40.70 % of the time. As there are six possible doubletons that West could hold, (QJ, Q3, Q2, J3, J2, 32), the chances that he will hold any particular doubleton are one-sixth of 40.70% which is 6.78%.

One question that I am frequently asked is, "What are my chances of picking up thirteen spades?" Even this could be worked out on the wooden tray. Simply add twenty-six more holes for the North-South cards and the chances of getting all thirteen spades are:

$$\frac{13}{52} \times \frac{12}{51} \times \frac{11}{50} \times \frac{10}{49} \times \frac{9}{48} \times \frac{8}{47} \times \frac{7}{46} \times \frac{6}{45}$$

$$\frac{5}{44} \times \frac{4}{43} \times \frac{3}{42} \times \frac{2}{41} \times \frac{1}{40}$$

We need a computer for this. The answer is: You will hold thirteen spades once in every 635,013,559,600 deals.

Infinitely more remote are the chances of all four players each holding a thirteen-card suit. This occurs once in every 2,235,197,406,895,366,368,301,560,000 deals. It is difficult to begin to comprehend such a number. Imagine that the entire population of the world were to sit down and play bridge continuously day and night without stopping. Once in every 100,000,000,000,000 years, on average, someone would deal this perfect hand.

This is why experts put so little faith in the newspaper reports, every year or so, that someone dealt a perfect hand. Where do these reports come from? Let me tell you a true story.

Many years ago my father was strolling on the deck of a ship and saw four passengers playing bridge. As he passed the table he calmly picked up the spare deck of cards, carried it to the rail, and quickly sorted it. He then replaced the cards, still unobserved by the players, and mingled with the other passengers at the far end of the deck to await developments.

The outcry was not long in coming and the excitement was tremendous. The story hit all the newspapers. And the four players, well-respected members of society, all swore that no one had tampered with the cards!

The Theory of Restricted Choice

One of the least-understood concepts in bridge is what is called the theory of restricted choice. The basic idea was first described by my husband, Alan Truscott, in a magazine article almost half a century ago.

Let's look again at Problem 2:

NORTH (DUMMY)

9 8 7 6

SOUTH (YOU)

A K 10 5 4

Assume that you lead the ace, on which West drops the jack. Is this more likely to be singleton? Or is it more likely that West holds the queen-jack doubleton? If it is a singleton, you should go to dummy and take a second-round finesse. And if it is from queen-jack doubleton, you should just lay down the king.

As we determined earlier, when the queen, jack, three and two are missing, West can be expected to hold the queen-jack alone 6.78% of the time.

To discover the probability of West holding the singleton jack and East the queen-three-two we could drop four more marbles. But we have a table handy, and it is easier to look up the 3-1 distribution. When four cards are missing a 3-1 distribution occurs 49.74 % of the time, and in half these cases it will be West who has the singleton: So the chance that West will hold a singleton is 24.87%. As there are four possible singletons, any particular singleton will occur in one quarter of these cases. Thus the chance that West will be dealt the singleton jack is 6.22%. Check this with the marbles if you wish.

As the probability that West will hold the doubleton queen-jack is 6.78% and the probability that he will hold any particular singleton is 6.22%, it may appear that the slightly better play is to lead out the ace and king.

This is not the right answer, however. In fact the second-round finesse is almost twice as good. Why? The answer to this and many related problems lies in the theory of restricted choice.

The reasoning behind restricted choice is this. If West held the doubleton queen-jack he would play either card at random because he knows they are equals. About half of the time he could be expected to play the queen and half of the time the jack. He would play the jack from queen-jack doubleton half of 6.78% or 3.39% of the time. Thus the second-round finesse is almost twice as good a play.

If this explanation is not entirely clear, let's try using a can of paint.

Remember, in this problem the queen and jack are equal. So imagine that before any cards are played declarer voluntarily closes his eyes and an impartial observer removes the queen and jack from wherever they are in the opponents' hands, and paints the faces of both cards so that no one can tell them apart. For convenience we will have him put an identical H (for honor) in the corner of each. Then he replaces the cards as they were in the East-West hands. Declarer opens his eyes and leads the ace, on which West drops an H.

Does West hold the doubleton HH, which as we have seen occurs 6.78% of the time? Or does he hold a singleton H? Remember that any particular singleton occurs 6.22% of the time. There are now two singleton Hs that West could hold, so the 6.22% becomes 12.44%. Thus the chances that the card played on the ace was a singleton H are almost twice that of its being from a doubleton HH. Obviously, the second-round finesse is the right play.

In real life there is no impartial observer to paint the cards for us. But a second-round finesse is still almost twice as good a play. Always think about the original distributions.

The bottom line: When the fall of an opponent's card provides you with an unexpected finesse possibility, it is usually right to take it.

If you have followed this chapter, you have grasped two of the most difficult concepts in bridge. Thanks to a wooden tray, some marbles, and a can of paint.

15

Tips for Experts or Near Experts Only

Splinter Bids Extended

Many players use splinter bids only in responding to major suits. (See chapter 11). They may not realize that splinter bids can be even more effective after minor openings.

WEST	EAST
1♣	3♠
?	

Instead of the normal choice between game or slam in the agreed suit, West has to consider notrump. About half the time that you open with a minor and partner has the equivalent of a forcing raise, the hand belongs in three notrump.

WEST	EAST	WEST	EAST
♠ K Q 10	♠ 8	1♣	3♠
♥ A 10 4	♥ J 8 7	3NT	
♦ 8 7	♦ A K J 9		
♣ A 8 6 4 3	♣ K 10 9 4 2		

Here West bids three notrump because he has so much strength wasted opposite East's singleton. But exchange West's major suit holdings and six clubs becomes an excellent contract. The key to West's decision lies in the ability to locate the singleton.

The splinter after a minor suit does not come up as often as over a major, but when it does it is more precise. In the example hand, East's three-spade bid shows a singleton (or void) spade, usually five-card club support, and it denies a four-card major. By far the most likely distribution is 1-3-4-5.

A singleton in the other minor is even rarer because it guarantees at least six trumps for partner.

WEST	EAST	WEST	EAST
♠ K Q 8 4	♠ A 8 6	1♣	3♦
♥ 5	♥ A 6 2	?	
♦ 9 8 5 2	♦ A		
♣ A K 7 5	♣ 9 8 6 4 3 2		

East cannot have a four-card major. Thus he must have at least six clubs. If West can locate three aces in partner's hand he can bid the grand slam with only 12 opposite 12.

WARNING: After a diamond opening bid the splinter in clubs would be 4♣. As this bypasses three notrump it should rarely be employed at matchpoints.

Here is another splinter to consider.

WEST	EAST
1♣	1♠
3♥ or 4♥	

Today a rebid of two hearts by West would be forcing because it is a reverse. This leaves both three hearts and four hearts as meaningless bids which might as well be splinters. Four hearts should be the stronger hand worth about twenty points in support of spades. Three hearts should be a mini-splinter worth only about seventeen, with the possibility of putting on the brakes in three spades. As two diamonds by West would also be a reverse, three diamonds and four diamonds should also be splinters.

When Opponents Interfere with Blackwood

Look at the following hand.

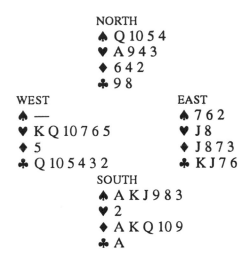

```
                    NORTH
                    ♠ Q 10 5 4
                    ♥ A 9 4 3
                    ♦ 6 4 2
                    ♣ 9 8
      WEST                          EAST
      ♠ —                           ♠ 7 6 2
      ♥ K Q 10 7 6 5                ♥ J 8
      ♦ 5                           ♦ J 8 7 3
      ♣ Q 10 5 4 3 2                ♣ K J 7 6
                    SOUTH
                    ♠ A K J 9 8 3
                    ♥ 2
                    ♦ A K Q 10 9
                    ♣ A
```

North-South are vulnerable. South deals.

SOUTH	WEST	NORTH	EAST
2♣	2♥	Pass	Pass
2♠	3♣	3♠	4♣
4NT	7♣	Pass	Pass
?			

You are South and well on your way to a vulnerable grand slam (worth 2210), when West throws a spanner into the "Blackworks" with a premature sacrifice. Do you double for a paltry 500-point set, or do you gamble that partner has an ace and bid seven spades?

There are several agreements that a pair can make and the simplest is this:

When an opponent interferes with Blackwood, responder should alternately double or pass as follows:

> With no aces, double.
> With one ace, pass.
> With two aces double.
> With three aces, pass.
> With four aces, double.

159

It is easy to remember that the double shows no aces, because logically if you have no aces you are least interested in proceeding with any slam effort, and most inclined to double the opponents.

The agreement has since become known as DEPO, (Double with Even, Pass with Odd). A variation, employed at the five-level, is often called D0P1, (Double with zero, pass with one, make the cheapest bid with two, etc.)

When a trump suit has been agreed, it is sensible to count the king of trumps as an ace, making five aces in all. The responses are the same.

On the example hand East should have bid five clubs at his second turn, not four clubs. This would have knocked out Blackwood entirely. As the auction went, however, North's pass over seven clubs should indicate one ace and South should have no trouble bidding seven spades.

The Cooperative Slam Double

SOUTH	WEST	NORTH	EAST
4♠	Dbl.	Pass	5♥
Pass	Pass	5♠	6♥
Pass	Pass	?	

East-West are vulnerable. You are North and hold:

♠ K 7 4   ♥ A 7   ♦ J 9 7 2   ♣ Q 7 5 3

Your partner deals and opens four spades. West doubles and East bids five hearts. This gets passed around to you and you take out insurance with five spades. Now East tries six hearts which is again passed around to you. What do you do?

The trouble here is that partner could easily have a trick in which case six hearts is going down. If partner has no cashing trick it is important to sacrifice. You need a cooperative slam double to sort out the difference.

The following method of using the cooperative slam double varies slightly from other methods in use. It is based on the logical agreement that when it is not clear whether or not to sacrifice against a slam, the player in LAST seat should pass if he has two defensive tricks, to be sure of playing it there. If he expects the opponents to make their contract, (i.e. he has no defensive tricks), he should sacrifice. If he has one defensive trick, he should double. Partner will pass if he can contribute one trick. Otherwise he will sacrifice.

As a corollary, the player in FIRST seat must double immediately with two defensive tricks, to prevent his partner from sacrificing. With one or no defensive tricks he should pass.

In a Nutshell

In FIRST seat, double with two tricks. Pass with one or no tricks.

In LAST seat, pass with two tricks, double with one trick, and sacrifice with no tricks.

In the example hand North should double to indicate exactly one defensive trick, and South will be able to make the final decision.

Other Responses to the Grand Slam Force

WEST	EAST
1♥	3♥
5NT	?

With two of the top three honors East naturally bids seven hearts. (See chapter 11). But what does he do if he does not have two of the top three? What do bids of six clubs, six diamonds and six hearts mean? It would obviously be extravagant to use all of these to deliver the same message: "I do not have two of the top three honors, partner."

The method which fits in most logically with modern bidding theory is to bid six of the agreed trump suit with the worst possible holding. In this case, with J x x x or worse bid six hearts. With Q x x x bid six diamonds. And with K x x x or A x x x bid six clubs. Note that when considering a grand slam the ace and king of trump are almost equally indispensable. But the queen is not. In the example above the hands might be:

161

WEST	EAST	WEST	EAST
♠ —	♠ K J 6 5	1♥	3♥
♥ K 8 6 5 4 2	♥ A 10 9 3	5NT	6♣
♦ A 2	♦ Q 8 5	7♥	Pass
♣ A K Q 9 8	♣ 3 2		

East's jump to three hearts shows four trumps and 10-12 points. West uses the grand slam force and East bids six clubs showing K x x x or A x x x. This allows West to bid seven missing the queen of trumps.

Note that over East's bid of six clubs there is a little room left for exploration. On some hands West could bid six diamonds to ask if East by any chance had an extra trump.

16

Bridge Tales

When bridge-players get together, they entertain one another with stories about hands. In the belief that every book should have some entertainment value, this chapter is devoted to amusing hands from real life.

The best hand I ever held, and also one of the most frustrating, occurred in a rubber bridge game. It was at the old Cavendish Club, which for 66 years was the home of many great players. My partner was the late Harry Fishbein, famous major-domo of the Mayfair Club. Vulnerable against non-vulnerable opponents, I picked up the following incredible collection:

♠ A K Q J 5 2   ♥ —   ♦ A K Q 10 8 7 3   ♣ —

It's hard to imagine that anything tragic could happen to this beauty, isn't it?

By the way, we didn't just play for peanuts in that game, and even if we did a vulnerable grand slam comes to a heck of a lot of peanuts!

The late Sam Stayman, on my right, dealt and opened three hearts. Now if I had had an average partner I would have just picked a suit and bid a grand slam myself. With an expert for a partner, however, I knew I could find out which suit was better, so I bid four hearts. My left-hand opponent passed, Fishy jumped to six clubs, and Stayman passed.

This development did not worry me. After all, I held the spade suit and could always bid seven spades if the bidding got out of control. So I bid six hearts to force Fishy to bid another suit. Do you see any danger in this, playing with an expert? I did not. In fact, I was mentally patting myself on the back for handling the situation so adroitly when catastrophe struck. Over six hearts Fishy inadvertently bid six diamonds!

Of course, the opponents kindly pointed out that six diamonds was insufficient. Under the laws Fishy could either make the bid sufficient in the same suit in which case there would be no penalty, or he could substitute any other sufficient call, in which case his *PARTNER WOULD BE BARRED FROM THE BIDDING.*

Fishy naturally hated to bid seven diamonds. (He had only a small doubleton.) So he corrected the bidding to six notrump and I was barred from the auction with the best hand I had ever seen!

It seems funny now, but imagine how I felt having to lay that hand down as dummy in six notrump.

There was a silver lining. Fishy held:

♠ 7 4   ♥ A 9 6 5   ♦ 5 4   ♣ K J 9 5 2

Both my suits broke, so he made six notrump easily. But of course either seven spades or seven diamonds would have been laydown.

*   *   *

In contrast, here is an example of a terrible hand that turned out to be lucky. Playing in the National Women's Pairs with Sylvia Stein of Detroit, I found myself looking at this gem:

♠ 7 4 2   ♥ 6 5 4   ♦ 6 5 3 2   ♣ 4 3 2

This was the worst hand I have ever held. Neither side was vulnerable, and Sylvia dealt and bid two clubs, strong and artificial. I responded two diamonds, negative, and the bidding went two spades on my left, pass, pass, back to me. What should I do next?

NORTH	EAST	SOUTH	WEST
(Sylvia)		(Me)	
2♣	Pass	2♦	2♠
Pass	Pass	?	

Interesting problem, isn't it? I obviously could not pass when Sylvia had opened the bidding with two clubs. But what would be the weakest bid I could make at this point? I finally decided to double, which turned out to be right. The complete deal was:

NORTH
♠ 8 3
♥ A K Q
♦ A K 9
♣ A K J 8 7

WEST
♠ A K Q J 10
♥ 10 8 7 3
♦ 10 4
♣ 9 6

EAST
♠ 9 6 5
♥ J 9 2
♦ Q J 8 7
♣ Q 10 5

SOUTH
♠ 7 4 2
♥ 6 5 4
♦ 6 5 3 2
♣ 4 3 2

Two spades doubled went for 300, which gave us a top because North-South had no game. Notice that Sylvia had made an excellent pass over two spades. Most players would automatically have bid three clubs.

* * *

Neither vulnerable:

NORTH
(Me)
♠ Q 8
♥ 10 6 3
♦ A Q J 9 6
♣ A Q 4

WEST
(Stayman)
♠ 5 4 3
♥ A 8 5
♦ K 5 3 2
♣ 10 5 2

EAST
(Mitchell)
♠ J 10 7 2
♥ K Q 7 4
♦ 10 8 7
♣ 7 6

SOUTH
(Becker)
♠ A K 9 6
♥ J 9 2
♦ 4
♣ K J 9 8 3

165

My favorite partner in the sixties was the late, great B. J. Becker. We won three major national titles together, and were silver medalists in the 1965 world team championships. This sensational deal, played against Sam Stayman and Victor Mitchell, occurred in the 1963 International Team Trials in Miami Beach.

The bidding:

SOUTH	WEST	NORTH	EAST
1♣	Pass	1♦	Pass
1♠	Pass	3♣*	Pass
4♣	Pass	4♠	Pass
6♣	Pass	Pass	Pass

* (In those days it was standard to play all jumps by responder as forcing.)

For some obscure reason, we had just decided to use Gerber over minor suits as well as notrump. When Becker bid four clubs, however, he had forgotten about this. Unfortunately I remembered, and bid four spades to show two aces. This was long before alerting was introduced.

Assuming my four-spade bid was natural, Becker read me for a singleton heart and leaped happily to six clubs. A person who bids two suits and jumps in a third suit is supposed to have at most a singleton in the fourth suit.

Stayman had also heard this strong bidding and decided to attack with a diamond lead. Believe it or not, the hand could no longer be defeated thanks to my *SIX* of hearts! Interchange my six with Stayman's five and the contract can not be made.

Although my dummy horrified Becker, he maintained his usual poker face and calmly finessed the diamond jack. He then cashed the diamond ace, throwing a heart, and ruffed a diamond. He led a trump to the ace and ruffed another diamond, establishing dummy's queen. When he then cashed the king and queen of clubs the lead was in dummy in this position:

166

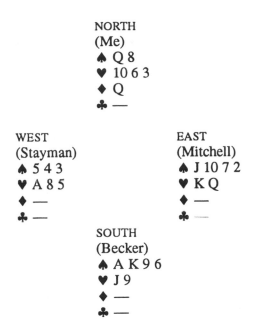

NORTH
(Me)
♠ Q 8
♥ 10 6 3
♦ Q
♣ —

WEST
(Stayman)
♠ 5 4 3
♥ A 8 5
♦ —
♣ —

EAST
(Mitchell)
♠ J 10 7 2
♥ K Q
♦ —
♣ —

SOUTH
(Becker)
♠ A K 9 6
♥ J 9
♦ —
♣ —

Becker now led the good diamond queen, on which East had to throw a heart honor. South threw the heart nine, and Stayman parted with a spade. Becker cashed the spade queen, and led the spade eight, forcing Mitchell to cover with the ten.

Becker won with king and led his heart jack! The defenders were through! If West ducked, East would win and have to lead a spade away from his jack-seven into declarer's ace-nine. And if West rose with the ace, he would have to lead away from his eight-five of hearts into my ten-six.

The defenders were in a state of shock at the end of the hand, and you can not blame them. Mitchell kept muttering, "He couldn't have done it without the six of hearts."

"Without the six of hearts," responded Becker solemnly, "we naturally wouldn't have bid so much!"

* * *

One of the silliest mistakes I ever made occurred on this hand from the 1964 Nationals in Portland, Oregon.

167

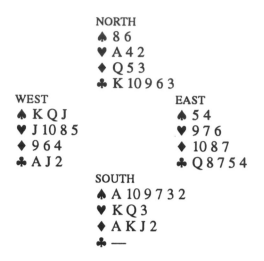

NORTH
♠ 8 6
♥ A 4 2
♦ Q 5 3
♣ K 10 9 6 3

WEST
♠ K Q J
♥ J 10 8 5
♦ 9 6 4
♣ A J 2

EAST
♠ 5 4
♥ 9 7 6
♦ 10 8 7
♣ Q 8 7 5 4

SOUTH
♠ A 10 9 7 3 2
♥ K Q 3
♦ A K J 2
♣ —

I was South, and when I picked up my hand the cards were already sorted for me. Unfortunately, three of the spades had been placed between the red suits and as I glanced at my hand I saw:

♠ A 10 9   ♥ K Q 3   ♠ 7 3 2   ♦ A K J 2

I bid one notrump with this "balanced" hand. Partner raised me to two notrump, and remembering my 17 points I bid three notrump without looking back at my cards. It was not until West had led the spade king and the dummy came down that I noticed I was a bit short in the club department. However, I won the spade and returned a spade, eventually making five notrump. I lost only two spade tricks and our score of 460 was a top on the board, since the field was in four spades making five for a score of 450.

Imagine how annoyed West was to find he had lost his ace of clubs on this auction! Yes, I was embarrassed!

*　　*　　*

The next hand is a horrible disaster, which I shall never forget because of the lambasting I got from my partner, the late, great John Crawford. This happened in the National Mixed Pairs in my first full year of national play and I was an unknown. In spite of the fact that we had never played together before, things went well. Going into the final session we were lying second in the field. We were seated North-South at Table One, and because my partner was one of the biggest names in bridge, we had a large ring of kibitzers. On the very first board I made a terrible goof.

Neither vulnerable:

NORTH
(Crawford)
♠ K 5 4
♥ K 2
♦ Q J 10 6 5
♣ A K 5

WEST
♠ Q J 8 6
♥ Q J 10 6
♦ A K 9
♣ 8 6

EAST
♠ A 10 3
♥ A 9 8 7
♦ 8 7 3 2
♣ Q 2

SOUTH
(me)
♠ 9 7 2
♥ 5 4 3
♦ 4
♣ J 10 9 7 4 3

The bidding:

WEST	NORTH	EAST	SOUTH
1♦	Dbl.	Redbl.	2♣
Pass	3♣	3♦	Pass
Pass	Dbl.	Pass	4♣
Dbl.	Pass	Pass	Pass

When partner doubled three diamonds I got cold feet and pulled it to four clubs, which went for 500. Instead of a top, we obviously had a bottom. Partner was furious.

"Young lady, I don't want you ever to take me out of a penalty double again as long as you live," etc.

He went on ranting for several minutes. I held on tightly to the table and swore to myself that I would not open my mouth. The worst part was to see the kibitzers beginning to feel sorry for me after the tirade. What I felt like pointing out was that if he had only passed

169

three diamonds we would have had a tremendous board. We had created a situation in the bidding in which East-West had been talked out of their four-heart contract.

Any North-South plus was bound to be sensational. Naturally, partner was even more irritated because subconsciously he knew the fault was half his.

However, I realized that if I pointed out an error to a famous expert like himself in front of a ring of kibitzers, all hope of ever recovering partnership harmony would be gone forever. I kept saying to myself:

"What difference does it make if twenty kibitzers spend the rest of their lives thinking that you are a tongue-tied half-wit? The important thing is to win, and you can't win if you don't get your partner back into a good humor."

Finally the outburst subsided and we both picked up our cards for the second board in stony silence. I said, "Partner, I think you've got some more on your mind."

"As a matter of fact I do," and he went on for another minute or two.

When he ran out of words this time I said:

"You know I hate to start this next board until you've got it all off your chest."

Finally, he smiled. Everyone breathed a sigh of relief. Partnership harmony restored, we managed to avoid any other disasters and went on to win the championship. If any of those twenty kibitzers ever reads this, I am not really a helpless and tongue-tied female. It was all for the good of the cause.

*　　*　　*

I am frequently asked if woman's intuition helps at the bridge table. I don't know the answer. Here's the type of good play that looks like intuition. (Besides, I'm tired of writing about my mistakes.) See what you think.

North-South vulnerable:

```
                    NORTH
                    ♠ 8 6
                    ♥ K 10 8 6 5 2
                    ♦ 10 3
                    ♣ K Q 3
       WEST                        EAST
       ♠ K 3                       ♠ 10 9 7 6
       ♥ J                         ♥ Q 9 7 4
       ♦ A K J 8 7 5               ♦ 4
       ♣ 9 6 5 2                   ♣ J 10 7 4
                    SOUTH
                    ♠ A Q J 4 2
                    ♥ A 3
                    ♦ Q 9 6 2
                    ♣ A 8
```

The bidding:

SOUTH	WEST	NORTH	EAST
1♠	2♦	3♥	Pass
3NT	Pass	Pass	Pass

I was South on this deal from the 1964 Spingold Knockout Team Championship. West led the diamond king and continued with the ace on which East parted, somewhat reluctantly, with a club. West shifted to the heart jack, which I won with the ace.

If the hearts broke I was in good shape, so I naturally continued with a heart to the king. When West showed out, I could no longer bring in the heart suit and I had to rely on the spades. I had two heart tricks, three clubs and a diamond, so I needed three spade tricks. How should I play the spades?

I was sure that West held the spade king, for without an entry he would not have cashed the diamond ace: He would have shifted at the second trick and waited for his partner to gain the lead. But did he have two spades or three?

If he had three, I could take a spade finesse, or play the ace followed by the queen. But if he had a doubleton king, the finesse would be fatal. By the time I made three spade tricks, the defense would have two spades, two diamonds and a heart.

I did the right thing. I cashed the spade ace and led a small spade.

171

When West's king popped up, I claimed the rest, making an overtrick.

How did I know that West had K x in spades and not K x x? Because of East's slight reluctance to part with a club at trick two. If East had held five clubs, he could have spared one painlessly. And if he only had four clubs, he had to have four spades, leaving his partner with the doubleton king.

*   *   *

Teamwork

For 15 years my favorite partner was the late Emma Jean Hawes of Fort Worth, Texas. Together we won four world titles and nine national titles.

Both sides vulnerable.

```
                         NORTH
                         ♠ 8 7 4 3
                         ♥ 6 2
                         ♦ K J 10 4
                         ♣ 5 4 2
        WEST (D)                        EAST
        ♠ K J 9 6 5 2                   ♠ A Q
        ♥ 10 7 4 3                      ♥ Q
        ♦ A 8 6                         ♦ Q 9 7 3 2
        ♣ —                            ♣ 10 9 8 7 6
                         SOUTH
                         ♠ 10
                         ♥ A K J 9 8 5
                         ♦ 5
                         ♣ A K Q J 3
```

The bidding:

WEST	NORTH	EAST	SOUTH
2♠	Pass	Pass	4♥
Pass	Pass	Pass	

West led the spade six.

172

Emma Jean as West opened with a weak two-bid in spades, and after two passes South jumped to four hearts. He probably expected to have an easy time when dummy appeared.

I won the first trick with the spade ace and shifted to the club ten. Partner trumped declarer's ace and led the spade king. Declarer ruffed this and drew trumps. I knew that South started with five clubs and no more than one diamond. But poor Emma Jean had no way to know this and was in grave danger of ducking a diamond and letting declarer steal the king. So I threw the diamond queen away on the second round of hearts.

After drawing trump, South led his diamond. But with the queen gone, there was no longer any temptation to duck. Emma Jean grabbed the ace and led a spade, so declarer eventually lost a club for one down.

*   *   *

The hands that appeal to me most are those in which a player creates a huge profit out of practically nothing. Here is an example from a rubber bridge game at the old Cavendish Club. My partner, Al Roth, manufactured a tremendous swing in our favor just by listening to the opponents.

Both sides vulnerable:

```
                      NORTH
                      ♠ Q 9 8 5 4 2
                      ♥ K Q
                      ♦ 10 3
                      ♣ Q J 2
        WEST                          EAST
        ♠ J 10 7 3                    ♠ A K 6
        ♥ 5 4                         ♥ 9 7 6 3 2
        ♦ A Q J 6 2                   ♦ 8 4
        ♣ 7 6                         ♣ 5 4 3
                      SOUTH
                      ♠ —
                      ♥ A J 10 8
                      ♦ K 9 7 5
                      ♣ A K 10 9 8
```

The bidding:

SOUTH	WEST	NORTH	EAST
	(Roth)		(me)
1♣	Pass	1♠	Pass
2♣	Pass	2♠	Pass
2NT	Pass	3NT	Pass
Pass	Dbl.	Pass	Pass
Pass			

Roth doubled the final contract of three notrump even though he had only eight points and a partner who had never bid. His reasoning was this. Both North and South had tried to sign off below game, so their total assets figured to come to slightly less than 26 points. As he himself had only eight points, I must have the remainder. With the diamond suit banked over declarer, Roth could see a big profit if he could just find my entry.

And find it he did. After some thought he led the spade three. South expected Roth to have high cards for his double, so he played the spade queen and I won with the king. The declarer did not want to part with one of his nine winners so he threw a diamond.

I shifted to a diamond, and Roth won with the jack and led another spade. I won with the ace and led my remaining diamond, and we took the first nine tricks for a score of 1400. Very few players would have thought of doubling with Roth's cards, and most of them wouldn't have beaten three notrump anyway.

*　　*　　*

Every bridge player has a little larceny somewhere in his soul which makes a stolen contract much sweeter than one earned legitimately. Here is one of my favorites.

NORTH
♠ K Q 6 4
♥ Q 7 6
♦ 5 2
♣ K Q 6 3

WEST
♠ A 8 3 2
♥ 5 4
♦ J 10 9 7 6
♣ 7 2

EAST
♠ 10 9 7 5
♥ 10 3
♦ 8 4 3
♣ A J 10 5

SOUTH
♠ J
♥ A K J 9 8 2
♦ A K Q
♣ 9 8 4

The bidding:

SOUTH	WEST	NORTH	EAST
(me)		(Emma Jean)	
1♥	Pass	1♠	Pass
3♥	Pass	5♥	Pass
6♥	Pass	Pass	Pass

Opening lead: diamond jack

You may think that the auction leaves something to be desired. (Blackwood, for example.) However, the bidding is given as it actually occurred.

I won the opening diamond lead with the ace and led a heart to the queen. I led a low spade, hoping to steal the jack if East held the ace. Unfortunately, West produced the ace. Fortunately he returned a heart, not a club but I still had absolutely no play for 12 tricks.

So I decided to abandon the good spades in dummy and ran my red winners coming down to this position:

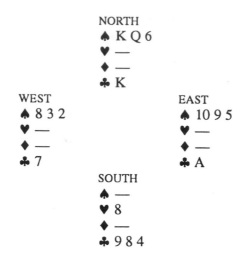

NORTH
♠ K Q 6
♥ —
♦ —
♣ K

WEST
♠ 8 3 2
♥ —
♦ —
♣ 7

EAST
♠ 10 9 5
♥ —
♦ —
♣ A

SOUTH
♠ —
♥ 8
♦ —
♣ 9 8 4

I led my last trump and threw the club king from the dummy. East could not imagine that I had no more spades. Who would deliberately abandon two winners in the dummy? So, clinging grimly to his spade stopper he discarded the club ace and I won the last three tricks with the nine-eight-four of clubs.